The Management of Change: Perspectives and Practice

The Management of Change: Perspectives and Practice

Audley Genus

INTERNATIONAL THOMSON BUSINESS PRESS
I T P® An International Thomson Publishing Company

London • Bonn • Boston • Johannesburg • Madrid • Melbourne • Mexico City • New York • Paris
Singapore • Tokyo • Toronto • Albany, NY • Belmont, CA • Cincinnati, OH • Detroit, MI

The Management of Change: Perspectives and Practice

Copyright © 1998 Audley Genus

First published by International Thomson Business Press

Business Press is a division of Thomson Learning. The Thomson Learning logo is a registered trademark used herein under license.

British Library Cataloguing-in-Publication Data
A catalogue record for this book is available from the British Library

First edition 1998
Reprinted 2000

Typeset by Columns Design Ltd, Reading
Printed in the UK by The Alden Group, Oxford and Northampton

ISBN 1-86152-047-6

Thomson Learning
Berkshire House
168–173 High Holborn
London WC1V 7AA
UK

http://www.thomsonlearning.co.uk

This book is dedicated to the memory of Etta Eunice Brown

Contents

List of case studies

List of figures

List of tables

Acknowledgements

I would like to thank so many people for their help and support during the preparation of this book. What follows is but a small selection of those individuals. This manuscript would not have materialized without the insights and criticism of colleagues and students within the Department of Management Studies at Brunel. In particular, the many hours of conversation I shared with the late John Quinn, about strategy, decision-making and a great deal else besides, deserve a special though sadly inadequate mention. Among my other colleagues Martin Harris and Ian McLoughlin have helped to improve my appreciation of some of the implications of technological innovation for the management of change within the workplace. John Howells and Keith Dickson have made a similar contribution with regard to my understanding of the strategic implications of innovation and operational technology. And, finally, to Professor David Sims and Professor Adrian Woods – I could not write once about the symbolic or story-telling aspects of strategy and change without thinking of you. On the editorial side, I would like to thank Steven Reed, my editor at International Thomson Business Press for his patience and support during the realization of this book. Its publication has been smoothed greatly by the efforts of Jenny Clapham, the development editor and Penny Grose, the production editor.

PART I

PERSPECTIVES OF CHANGE

INTRODUCTION: PERSPECTIVES OF MANAGING CHANGE 1

INTRODUCTION

Some time ago I was talking with a visitor to the Department of Management Studies at Brunel University. He wanted to know why I was bothering with the production of yet another book on the management of change. After all, the shelves of libraries and bookshops alike are replete with slim and not-so-slim texts on the same subject are they not? This chapter provides an extended version of the reply that was given that day and in so doing explains the raison d'être for this particular project. This introduction also serves to identify the main concerns that are to be addressed in the subsequent pages and chapters of this volume; a simple organizing framework is developed to enable the reader to make sense of the range and interconnectedness of the issues and concepts in question.

This book is something of a hybrid. It has its origins in two aspects of my experience of lecturing and researching strategic management, decision-making and operations management. One of these relates to the need to ensure that students taking courses in the management of change at final year undergraduate or postgraduate (MSc/MBA) level have the required grasp of the fundamental concepts of strategic management. In particular, there is an absence of appropriate texts for students taking advanced courses in managing change who have not previously studied strategy at introductory or intermediate levels. This is revealed in a gap between the introductory textbooks on strategic management, of either the comprehensive or 'essence of' variety, and the dedicated volumes on the management of change, embracing the written up research on the topic. One should note in the latter category also those contributions which form part of series of books aimed at delivering a multidisciplinary approach to understanding change. In one sense, therefore, the writing of this book is motivated by a wish to avoid assuming the reader's prior knowledge, whilst at the same time affording detailed discussion of research in the area.

On the second point the author is struck by the insights into the management of change which may be derived from a range of academic disciplines. The problem is to select from and then mould disparate contributions into an integrated whole, while adhering to the task of illuminating the core themes and issues bearing on the subject under review. Subsequent sections of this chapter will have more to say about the organization of the book and the material within it. For now, one may single out the contention that major organizational change occurs through the planned strategic decisions of (senior) managers which are then translated into operational actions. This is a commonly enough held view of change implicit in much of the output of management gurus and, in general, that of those with a less than critical orientation to the subject.

Due contemplation of this conventional view of change provides the sort of integrating themes just mentioned which may benefit from a multidisciplinary approach. For example, to what extent do managers exercise strategic choice, rather than merely reacting to the demands of external environmental contingencies? How deliberately planned (or 'plannable') is fundamental change, as exemplified by major restructuring, re-engineering or total quality programmes? Indeed, how 'major' or 'strategic' are such moves in concept and in application? And what are the roles of top management, other managers and non-managerial groups in all of this? These and other related questions suggest the central issues with which subsequent chapters are concerned. Before attending to such matters, however, more needs to be done by way of setting the orientation of the book.

A NEW PARADIGM?

At the core of this book are two competing observations. The first of these concerns the argument that over recent decades industrialized economies have been the subject of changing patterns of consumption and production. This process has occurred to such an extent that contemporary forms of organization, now being seen as representing 'best practice', are more appropriately described as 'post-Fordist' (or post-industrial). Explaining the transition to the new paradigm has typically involved reference to a number of factors. These include a decline in mass consumer markets, standard products with predictable demand and long production runs, and a rise in more fragmented, differentiated markets and short production runs. Also, the increasing significance of services compared to manufacturing (as reflected in changes in their relative share of economic output and employment) is argued. Other pertinent contributory factors include the increasing extent and intensification of internationalized competition, the globalization of production and marketing, and the emergence and accelerated development of communications, information and production technology. Meanwhile, the national economies of the industrialized countries have become progressively intertwined and characterized by periodic and unpredictable bouts of growth and deep recession. And finally, in a number of countries governments of the Left and Right alike have followed policies to 'roll back the frontiers of the state'. This has seen them withdraw from interventionist approaches to managing economy and industry, privatize formerly nationalized industries, and introduce marketization in remaining publicly owned activities. Further, whole sectors have been deregulated (such as the UK financial services industry) and employment legislation enacted in the name of removing existing rigidities and so enhancing the flexibility of labour.

Indeed, flexibility is a key word. The developments described in the previous paragraph have been argued to necessitate or enable the flexible forms and processes of organization associated with the emerging post-Fordist paradigm. Essentially, old certainties have been superseded by new and continuing uncertainties which make flexibility a desirable capability. So, the archetypal post-Fordist organization is that which has made the most of flexible technology, labour and related forms of control and co-ordination. And, in uncertain environments, this will be in pursuit of enhanced product innovation and differentiation, while at the same time attending to the quality and efficiency of production (in effect, resolving what Abernathy [1978] calls the 'productivity dilemma'). What is more, the focus of such change is not merely with the internal workings of organizations, since the notion of post-Fordism also brings into question their relations with external parties. The internal aspect of post-Fordist organization addresses the nature of corporate restructuring, delayering and team-building, rather than the celebration of vertical integration, hierarchy, and specialization of work associated with the Fordist mode. The external aspect, by contrast, concerns the development of supplier relationships or outsourcing of non-core activities, for example. Developments in these areas bring into question issues of trust, the nature of contracting and the definition of organizational boundaries, some of which have been explored by invoking the concept of strategic networks.

At this point a second set of observations and arguments may be brought into play. These assert that the terms 'post-Fordism', 'post-industrialism' and 'flexibility' are ill-defined and rhetorical and that a longer-term historical perspective would reveal how 'Fordism' has been misread in any case (Jacques, 1990; Pollert, 1991). An example of the type of confusion that exists with regard to the new labels concerns the scope of the changes analysed and prescribed. Thus, as mentioned above, some commentators speak of the emergence of a new paradigm. Here, what is being referred to are radical developments in technology and economic organization. These make possible or even necessitate novel methods of organizing at the level of the firm, such that the latter take on the status of a new conventional wisdom. Yet the same terms are employed when many changes that are much narrower in scope are advanced or realized.

Pollert (1991) comments on the slippery nature of the concept of flexibility, which is applied indiscriminately to changes in employee relations practices, production systems and universal transformation in organizational form alike. Further, there are national differences in usage of the notion, so that in France and the UK, for example, labour market flexibility is associated with fixed-term contracts and the facility with which employees may be hired or laid off. However, in Sweden and Germany, the same term is more closely identified with the development of a skilled, well-qualified labour force.

Following a different line of argument there are those who have questioned the emergence of a 'post-industrial' paradigm, on the grounds that such a view exaggerates the decline of manufacturing. Although the statistics for employment seem to indicate clearly the new significance of service sector activity and high-technology 'sunrise' enterprises, these may be misleading. What is being neglected is the linkage between manufacturing (tangible) and services (intangible) (Cohen and Zysman, 1994). So, this interdependence needs to be acknowledged and may be thought of in terms of Quinn's work on 'intelligent enterprises'. Here, (in part) he describes the complementarity and co-ordination of services, knowledge management and production activities (Quinn, 1992; cf. Teece's [1987] notion of complementary assets).

Another point of issue is taken by Jaques (1990) who ponders on the benefits of hierarchy. The new prescription for organization that emphasizes delayering and autonomous teams, *inter alia*, is wrong according to Jacques. Yes, there are drawbacks to hierarchy and some of these have been properly identified, such as the lack of added value associated with excessively tall organizational hierarchies and what Kanter (1983) refers to as the 'elevator mentality' of large corporations so structured. Yet, Jaques argues, there is virtue in hierarchy (a term which he says should not be confused with 'bureaucracy'). For example, contrary to the argument for blurred job descriptions, team-working and rewards, and matrix mechanisms (cf. Kanter 1983), hierarchical forms of organizing facilitate the specialization of mental work which is subject to discontinuities. In this way, employees with the appropriate expertise may be placed within the relevant layer in the hierarchy (the Peter principle notwithstanding). Further, the employment of hierarchies also helps to specify the scope and time duration of accountability for work. This is important to the extent that so-called post-Fordist forms of organizing emphasize a collective approach to work, whilst employment and reward continue predominantly on the basis of individual labour contracts and effort.

Fundamentally, a point of issue that pervades the chapters of this book turns on the claim that 'despite the potential benefits of flexibility, [there has not been] a wholesale shift in the behaviour of firms' (Starkey *et al.*, 1991: 165). Much of what follows is concerned with inertia, continuity and the difficulties of change towards the prescribed organizational forms indicated in this section. This is balanced by attention to manifestations of change that do seem to have occurred in the direction of the new paradigm, mindful of how illusory or contradictory these can be compared to the ideal types to be found in the literature. The next section further outlines the general orientation of the book with reference to a range of theoretical and methodological perspectives, contemplation of which will help to provide a framework for analysing and understanding the subject matter to follow.

Voluntarism⋯⋯⋯⋯Week voluntarism/soft determinism⋯⋯⋯⋯Environmental
                                                                       determinism

Figure 1.1   Perspectives of managing change.

PERSPECTIVES OF CHANGE

Essentially, there are three generic perspectives of the occurrence of change. Within and between these perspectives the basic premises of the range of literature related to the management of change may be located. At root these perspectives are based on different guiding assumptions concerning the relative influence of human discretion and action on the one hand, and environmental exigencies on the other, upon organizational change. The three perspectives may be thought of in terms of a continuum (see Figure 1.1). At one end of such a continuum is placed a perspective labelled 'voluntarism', at the opposite end is located 'environmental determinism' and in the middle range 'weak voluntarism' (or 'soft determinism') might be an appropriate rubric.

Each of these categories embraces ways of looking at organizations and change having certain shared fundamental orientations. In helping to define the distinctions between the perspectives certain key issues are called upon with which, implicitly or explicitly, approaches to strategic decision-making and change must be concerned. These are:
1. **Issues of context and uncertainty**, linked to questions of the 'why' of change and the way in which the external environment is conceived.
2. **Issues of content and scale**, in other words the 'what' of change, connected to how fundamental (or strategic) relevant decisions are and the implications of the scale of choice.
3. **Issues of process**, linked to questions of the leadership of change, commitment to and participation in organizational decision-making and the portrayal of objectives and values.
4. **Issues of method**, where the question of what time frame is applied to understanding change arises, and so, too, do more general questions about the nature of organizations and research. These include questions of the degree to which research about organizational change adopts a machine metaphor or functionalist view of organizations compared to a holographic (learning) or interpretive approach. (Much more on these issues of method will appear throughout the book. The above list may be compared to the content-context-process framework presented in Pettigrew and Whipp [1991: 26].)

Consider first the perspective termed 'voluntarism'. This perspective privileges the choice and discretion of the strategic decision-maker (and indeed, the individual decision-maker tends to be the focus of this general approach where the influence of neoclassical economics on strategic thought is most keenly felt). The voluntaristic perspective is the domain of planned views of strategy and change. Here, the most influential schools of thought connected to strategic management and change may be identified, including the related design, planning and positioning schools (Mintzberg, 1990). Whatever the particular variant, contributors to the debate share a common philosophy, whether the writer concerned is Andrews (1987) on the design of strategy, Ansoff (1965) and Ansoff and McDonnell (1990) on a more elaborate planning approach, or Porter (1980; 1985) on strategy as positioning. The general orientation, characteristic of much of the work on strategy emanating from Harvard Business School, has dominated textbook writing, teaching and beliefs about the practice of strategy and change (Mintzberg, 1990).

There is a different wing of the voluntaristic perspective which is represented by those such as Tom Peters, who would consider their view of strategic change to be poles apart from that of the design, planning and positioning schools. Here, though, 'excellence' thinking may be thought of as emphasizing the role of organizational choice and, in particular, the role of strong leaders in shaping the destiny of the organizations they lead (Peters and Austin, 1985). As with the above, the focus of attention on this view tends to be on the dramatic turnaround and on the successes some exemplary organizations enjoy in achieving transformational change. Of course, Peters's work too has become a common feature of management teaching and, indeed, the wider popularization of management thought.

At the other end of the spectrum lies 'environmental determinism'. Within this generic perspective the dominant theme is that the discretion and choice that are so much to the fore in the voluntaristic perspective are severely constrained by environmental, including market, forces. This 'limits to choice' argument is most stringently developed within population ecology (Aldrich, 1979), although the ugly-sounding concept of institutional isomorphism also draws attention to external factors which shape organizational change (Powell and DiMaggio, 1991).

Population ecology approaches comprise two streams of thought regarding strategic choice and environmental determinism. These have been referred to as 'strict' population ecology on one hand (Clark and Staunton, 1993), and organizational ecology, emphasizing organizational adaptiveness and co-operation between firms on the other (Scott and Meyer, 1991). Informing this book is the latter, less restrictive view of population ecology. Decision-makers enjoy some discretion over organizational innovation and change, though clearly this is 'bounded'. They are not, however, merely at the mercy of events. Having said this, it is instructive to consider the more severe version of population ecology. Taking this view, an analogy with the natural selection model of biological ecology is made with reference to environmental factors which determine the survival or exit of organizations from the aggregate population. These factors are the external environment's selection criteria. According to Aldrich, resources are distributed unevenly in niches in the environment. Innovation occurs as organizational actors seek to improve their use of such resources but, in effect, they are acting 'blind'. They do not and cannot know the rules by which the environment selects, but the organization may survive to evolve from the serendipitous success of their decision-making. Central to understanding organizational change, therefore, is the force of broader ecological considerations which restrict strategic choice. A qualification to this is made to cater for the observation that the largest organizations enjoy a freer hand. Hence, Aldrich (1979) states that for most organizations there is little room for manoeuvre, such are the limits and constraints of environmental selection processes, but that the largest and most powerful organizations enjoy the luxury of strategic choice.

Although not neatly fitting under the rubric of environmental determinism there are other contributions to the literature which may be mentioned at this point which support a limited view of strategic choice. Cohen *et al*. (1972) develop a garbage-can model of organizational choice, for example. Here, the conception of organizational decision-making is captured by reference to 'organized anarchies'. Decision-making is a random activity subject to the vagaries of luck and timing. Ambiguity and dispute over organizational objectives further add to a picture of chaotic, rather than rationally planned, decision-making. In a similar vein, Stacey (1996) points to the nature of deterministic chaos in an application of chaos theory to strategic management and change. Conceiving of organizations as feedback systems in disequilibrium, Stacey is pessimistic about the capacity of organizations to be 'in control' in the long term – there is no way in which the future consequences and amplification of even small changes made now can be predicted with accuracy. However, small-scale changes take time to amplify. Therefore, there may be some point to near-term forecasting of how the system will behave and, thus, planned change over the shorter term may be feasible.

Between voluntarism and environmental determinism a category referred to as weak voluntarism/soft determinism has been identified. Here, the middle ground is steered between the centrality and latitude of human decision-making and the potency of environmental conditions, as indicated in the previous paragraph. Although this perspective comprises a number of distinct schools of thought with their own emphases and orientation, in general there is a bent for addressing the interplay between organizational activities and decision-making and environmental factors and awareness. Depending upon the specific variant under consideration, there is some attention within this perspective to the ebb and flow of the relative strength of organizational versus environmental factors influential on strategic decision-making and change. Fundamental is the notion of incrementalism. Charles Lindblom's (1959; 1979) work on an incremental approach to decision-making developed as a response to the inapplicability of 'rational' models, which neither adequately described nor usefully prescribed for 'real world' decision-making. In particular, such models were seen as being unsuited to analysing the content and process of decision-making in organizations operating in uncertain contexts. Instead, in these situations, ignorance of the consequences of alternative strategic choices and a lack of detailed information required to make rational (i.e. maximizing) decisions, leads to incremental, small-scale changes. Moreover, the prevalence of incremental processes for decision-making draws attention to the negotiation of organizational objectives. (These in the received view are given: profit maximization is assumed.)

Quinn's (1980; 1982) subsequent work on logical incrementalism uncovers how, in the large corporations he studied, commitment to fundamental change is moulded over a period of time, with senior managers seeking out the zones of indifference of potential recalcitrants. He also asserts some role for more formal planning approaches (which Lindblom does not, save for an oblique reference to 'strategic analysis', in his 1979 paper). These may contribute to the build-up of 'persuasive data' which may be employed to support particular strategies or, more generally, add to an organization's database of information on its market.

Lindblom and Quinn, and also Mintzberg in his work on emergent strategy-making (see the collection of articles in Mintzberg and Quinn, 1991) are primarily concerned with activities in public and private sector organizations in North America. In Britain the work of Pettigrew and Johnson, for example, has sought to improve our understanding of strategic change, based upon an incremental, emergent view of the process. They argue for a longitudinal approach to understanding change which enables the interplay of organizational and environmental factors to be appreciated within a temporal context, centred upon studies of change at ICI (Pettigrew, 1985) and Fosters, the clothing retailer (Johnson, 1987). As well as pressing the value of analysing the process of organizational change, within the context of the wider environment through time, questions of the subjective interpretation of 'environment', and their significance to managing change, also come to the fore (Pettigrew and Whipp, 1991). Advancing their claim for a new approach to corporate strategy Knights and Morgan (1991) suggest that strategy needs to be seen as more than can be explained either by rationalist accounts or by appeal to the interpretability of actors' frames of reference. Instead corporate strategy should be seen as discourses (ideas and practices) which 'transform managers and employees alike into subjects who secure their sense of purpose and reality by formulating, evaluating and conducting strategy' (Knights and Morgan, 1991: 252).

Following Foucault, corporate strategy as a 'discourse' refers both to ways of seeing (i.e. perspectives of) strategy and what people do, including the techniques they use, that together 'become part of the everyday reality of organizations' (Knights and Morgan, 1991: 259). Moreover, the pervasiveness of academic research and teaching on the subject, plus the emergence of a raft of consultants armed with the language and techniques of strategy, help to create a situation where the discourse of strategy becomes the legitimate form of reasoning about the nature of organizations and change. In doing so it displaces explanations of organizational change emanating from various other disciplines (or rather 'discourses'), while within organizations, those who do not share the dominant logic of strategy, or who do not possess the skills associated with the employment of its techniques, may be marginalized from debates about change.

Knights and Morgan state that conceiving of strategy as a discourse 'effects a more radical break with the orthodox rationalist view of strategy' than do processual approaches, which they consider still to adhere to the rationalist view that strategy 'exists to resolve problems *vis-à-vis* the organization and its environment' (1991: 267). To the extent that from Lindblom on incrementalism to Pettigrew on processualism, there has been a concern for how problems are constructed, rather than given, this seems a little harsh. Nevertheless, this view of strategy as a discourse draws attention to other types of explanation of organizational activity residing in different disciplines focusing on the actions of, and power relations between, the protagonists (and non-protagonists) in change. At the very least it acts as a kind of health warning about the subject and techniques of strategic management and its treatment of organizational change.

THE LAYOUT OF THE BOOK

This introduction forms the first of the four chapters making up Part I of this book. The role of this and the remaining chapters of Part I within the book as a whole is that of scene-setting. The primary objective is to introduce and to illuminate fundamental concepts, and in doing so to illustrate the practical implications for managing change. Thus Chapters 2 and 3 are founded upon an appreciation of the pervasiveness and limitations of concepts of strategic and structural fit. Notions of fit, of varying specification, dominate thinking about the management of change, and are presented or implied in treatments of change within different camps in the strategy field, or in the vast and disparate literatures connecting organizational and technical change. Given this book's general orientation, the preoccupation of Chapters 2 and 3 lies with the strategic management related literature, where the force of prescription about ideal organizational forms and practice is at its strongest, as represented by the literature on corporate excellence and the recommendations of various gurus on appropriate organizational forms to fit their view of contemporary competitive conditions.

Chapter 4 introduces a wider range of concepts pertinent to understanding change with a somewhat broader disciplinary base and arguably a greater concern for issues of time and a historical orientation for understanding management, strategy and behaviour in organizations. For example, the way in which flexibility is conceived, as a capability of good strategic decision-making but also as a controversial byword for contemporary organizational restructuring, attracts attention. Relatedly, the nature of knowledge creation and organizational learning and their significance to change and performance are topics which require some preparatory definition. In addition, the insights to be gained from work which may be categorized under the rubric of 'institutional' theories are addressed. The views in question embrace a range of thinking about organizations and change spanning economics-based and sociological treatments, and include the work of Williamson (1975) on the importance of transactions costs and contracting to decisions about the management of organizational hierarchies, or outsourcing, for example. Still with the more economics-oriented version of institutional theory in mind, the work of Nelson and Winter (1982) on organizational routines offers an approach from which to consider the retention of organizational memory. (This relates to how people in organizations build up expertise and experience which permits possibly difficult activities to be performed 'routinely' without having to go back to first principles each time.) By contrast, it also invites consideration of potential barriers to learning, since routines may be thought of as relatively difficult to undo. Further, a more sociological viewpoint takes us back towards the notion of population ecology by way of the concept of isomorphism. In this regard, the manner of the question being posed is to ask why organizations become alike in the things that they do, or the way that they do them, for example with respect to the vogue in recent years for introducing quality programmes, or re-engineering. To some extent answers to the question emphasize external drivers of choice and change, or at least subjective understanding of the 'world outside' which finds its way into organizational decision-making, rather than rational, purposive and strategic voluntary choice. As such, interpretive views of decision-making also require, and receive, some elucidation in Chapter 4.

In Part II there is a switch of focus. The fundamental concepts from the first part of the book are brought forward, but this time are applied to a contemplation of factors which, from a reading of the literature, appear central to the management of change. These factors entail concepts which require exposition, as did key ideas presented in Part I. For example, Chapter 5, in part, revisits earlier discussions of notions of fit. However, on this occasion there is rather more focus on the problem of conceiving 'environment' objectively. Rather more is developed from the standpoint of research subscribing to a subjective, interpretive notion of environment, recognizing the implications of this for the management of awareness of (the need for) change.

Chapters 6 and 7 both centre on aspects of the content of change (in rude terms the 'what' compared to Chapter 5's 'why'). The relevance of the assertion that organizations should change form and process to permit adaptation, and better still, flexibility and learning, in order to elicit a fit between organization and new external contingencies persists. The substance of these chapters is the implementation of organizational restructuring and new operational processes, incorporating various labels such as 'downsizing', 'empowerment', 'team-building', 'total quality management' and 'business process re-engineering', ideas about which are more debatable than the impression given by their proponents suggests. The nature and management of advanced computerized technology for realizing the 'new organization' is a contentious theme necessarily implicated in such a discussion. In particular, the exploitation of the 'informating' (Zuboff, 1988) capacity of information technology, compared to the efficiency benefits of automation, and what this means for the management of human capital and knowledge in organizations, come to the fore.

Finally, in Chapter 8, the vexing topic of leadership is the centrepiece. The reason for this lies in the preponderance of 'great man' stories in the literature, and especially in the popular literature, on the management of organizational turnarounds, for example. The heroic view of leading change directs attention to the individual chief executive and their prime role in particular episodes of crisis and transformation. What it tends to neglect is a more considered view of the context in which change occurs and the perspective which time lends to the balance and interplay between voluntaristic decision-making, organizational process and the whims of the world outside.

SUMMARY

In this introductory chapter the rationale and organization of this book have been explained. The production of another volume on the subject of change stems from a concern to develop an understanding and critique of the basic premises of the strategic management literature. Entwined with this is a willingness to illustrate some of the limitations of and opportunities for improving the strategy literature by embracing insights into the subject of change that have emerged from other academic disciplines, including mainstream organization theory, management of technology and innovation, human resource management and institutional economics. Three broad perspectives of change have been identified: voluntarism, which privileges strategic choice, weak voluntarism/soft determinism, and environmental determinism which imposes severe limits to strategic choice. A warning siren has been sounded regarding the pervasiveness of the discourse of strategy. Overall, the topics and concepts which best capture what this book is about are the transition to post-Fordist organizational forms, flexibility and the planning of change to ensure fit between aspects of organization and the external environment. Indeed, the next chapter now takes up the subject of fit in greater detail, focusing upon voluntarist approaches to the notion.

TEXTBOOK APPROACHES TO STRATEGIC CHANGE AND NOTIONS OF FIT

2

INTRODUCTION

Whether the stance taken as regards the sources of competitiveness accords with the strain of thinking inherent in the work of Michael Porter (i.e. from the 'positioning' school) or adopts the perspective associated with resource-based competition or the literature on corporate excellence, there is a degree of commonality concerning the significance of concepts of fit within the literature on strategy and change. This chapter identifies the classical notions of fit and considers the limitations of the conventional application of strategic fit to understanding more thoroughly the process of managing change (structural fit is accorded a similar treatment in Chapter 3). Historically, the field of strategic management has been influenced by the contribution of writers and researchers with a background in micro-economics. For example, the fundamental concept of competitive advantage is presented in the third section of this chapter as espoused in the work of one seminal thinker – Michael Porter – who exemplifies the approach of the positioning school to the formulation of strategy. The task of this section is to review, in part, this contribution in terms of its relevance to issues of implementation and change, topics which are not well addressed in the strategy mainstream. An ongoing argument of this chapter is that notions of strategic fit which pervade the literature do not serve well the requirements of researchers and practitioners alike when it comes to understanding or analysing the management of change. The next section provides an outline of what is meant by 'fit' and the general relevance of the concept to the subsequent discussion.

NOTIONS OF 'FIT'

Essentially, two basic notions of 'fit' relevant to the management of change are at issue in this chapter (and in Chapter 3): a) strategic fit; and b) structural (or cultural) fit.

The concept of strategic fit underlies much of contemporary writing on strategic management, whereby strategy is a means for achieving a match between the external environment of an organization and its internal capabilities, as part of the quest for establishing competitive advantage over rival competitors. Textbook treatments of the notion tend to express strategic fit in terms of a match between external opportunities and threats, and internal strengths and weaknesses (Hax, 1994: 8–12). More specifically, one may distinguish two aspects of strategic fit , or 'consonance', as Rumelt (1994: 188) terms it. The first of these concerns the 'basic mission or scope of the business' and may be viewed as being connected to the breadth of an organization's activities and boundaries, with the focus of the analyst being on general macro-economic, technological and socio-political trends. The second aspect refers to the fit between organizational strategy and factors at play within a more narrowly defined industrial or competitive scene. Here, as in the Porterian model, the actions of and relationships between existing and potentially new competitors, suppliers and buyers come to the fore. Such proponents of the industrial organization economics view stress the competitive positioning of firms within their sector, seeing strategic fit in terms of the development of a generic or competitive strategy which enables 'defendable' positions to be taken *vis-à-vis* identified industry trends and broader macro-level factors (cf. Porter, 1980; 1985). Referring to the 'design' school of strategic thinking, Mintzberg (1990) portrays the underlying approach reflected in the industrial organization economics view. Primary attention is directed to the analysis of the external and internal contexts of an organization, with the former revealing opportunities and threats and the latter strengths and weaknesses of the organization (here, issues linked to the internal appraisal may receive short shrift, as Mintzberg [1990] explains with reference to the work of Andrews, and rather scant attention is devoted to understanding managerial and employee values). Moreover, one of the basic premises is that the implementation of strategy follows the full formulation of strategy. In a manner redolent of Chandler's (1962) 'structure follows strategy' thesis the view is that structural issues connected to organizational change cannot be specified until the strategy of an organization has been decided and made explicit (Mintzberg, 1990).

The line of thinking represented by the positioning/design approach could be argued to contrast with resource-based (including 'excellence'-oriented) views of strategy which tend to emphasize the role of organizational resources in conferring advantageous capabilities which allow the rules of the competitive game to be reshaped by innovative organizations. At the risk of being glib, the positioning/design view takes an 'outside-in' view of strategic choice and fit, with organizations exercising strategic choice on the basis of their analysis of the external (and especially the industry environment) whereas the resource-based and excellence approaches take an 'inside-out' perspective where organizations' internal capabilities allow them to rewrite the rules of industry competition (de Wit and Meyer, 1994). The extent to which competing approaches actually share assumptions regarding strategic fit is another important issue to be addressed below.

As mentioned above, the dominant strain of thinking regarding strategic and structural issues has conceived of a separation between planning and doing, implementation being essentially relegated to a near-subordinate role compared to that of strategic analysis or choice. Still, where the matter of implementation and change do receive more explicit attention this is often with the aforementioned separation firmly intact. Organizational resources and structure are there to serve prior-made strategy; internal resource and structural configurations must be consistent with the chosen strategy and with each other. (Indeed, this all but defines 'structural fit' according to this tradition.)

The work of Chandler is apposite here. His seminal study (Chandler, 1962) of the historical evolution of strategy and structure in America's largest multinational corporations theorized that the structure of an organization follows its growth strategy. This 'structure-follows-strategy' thesis has become as debatable as it has been pervasive. The remainder of this section illustrates the theoretical underpinnings of this view of the strategy–structure relationship further.

The notion of structural fit has been developed to refer to two considerations: one involves the implementation of the most appropriate organizational structure for the product/market strategy in question; the other concerns the need to fit together dimensions of organizational structure so that they are compatible with each other, as well as with organizational strategy. As Galbraith and Kazanjian (1986: 109) put it, organizations: 'need to adopt an internally consistent set of practices in order to implement the product strategy effectively … In organizations, everything is connected to everything.'

Asserting the role of strategic choice of the dominant coalition in an organization, Child (1972) strove to ameliorate the determinism often associated with the research of certain contingency theorists concerning the sources of change in organizational structure. He asserts the exercise of voluntaristic strategic choice though not towards 'wholly predictable outcomes' (Child, 1997: 44). Applying aspects of this analysis to our present discussion enables some insight into the claimed appropriateness (or 'efficiency') of structural alternatives which Child considers in terms of their 'goodness of fit'. Attaining good 'fit' is viewed in terms of the establishment of 'structural arrangements … consistent with the scale and nature of operations planned' (Child, 1972: 17).

The contribution of contingency theory as presented in research undertaken by Burns and Stalker (1961), Lawrence and Lorsch (1967), Thompson (1967) and Woodward (1965), for example, was to identify determinants of changes in organization structure. These included environmental uncertainty, technology and the size of the organization but did not conceive of or admit any concept of an intervening variable of strategic choice. Thus the familiar accounts of structural change and conditions where goodness of fit could be attained asserted that:

- environmental uncertainty (understood in terms of degree of dynamism and complexity) required an organizational structure which could facilitate adaptability (i.e. 'organismic' rather than 'mechanistic' organizations, cf. Burns and Stalker, 1961)
- the technology of production determined organizational design such that high task specialization and tightly defined work roles, rules and routines would be effective for mass production technology but so not for small or unit batch technology organizations, where effectiveness is associated with relatively fewer levels of hierarchy and less specialization of management, and also greater professionalization of employees than in the mass production organization (Woodward, 1965)
- increases in the size of an organization dictate structural differentiation (e.g. through multidivisionalization) in the pursuit of effectiveness, though with consequences for the control and co-ordination of sub-units (Child, 1972, pulling together arguments from Weber, the Aston Studies research team and Blau on this issue).

If the determinism inherent in the above explanations of structural variation is softened by introducing the intervening variable of strategic choice, as did Child all those years ago, a somewhat clearer view of the activity of managing strategy and change emerges (unless, of course, one subscribes to the view that the environmental and other factors do 'determine' and, so, managers have little discretion over the various decision-making areas discussed in the foregoing). Now, factors such as organizational size or scope and operational technology may be seen as representing 'multiple points of reference' (Child, 1972: 15) or landmarks for strategic decision-making. This in turn refers to the process (analytically or politically understood) by which organizational objectives, goals and values come to be selected on the basis of some understanding or perception of the nature of conditions in the organization's wider environment, as well as of that organization's place and ability to prosper within that context. In asserting the role of strategic choice as described above, Child considers that this factor is the 'direct source of variation in formal structural arrangements' (Child, 1972: 16) in a process which occurs along lines familiar to students of textbook strategy (see Figure 2.1). Here, Child's model of the process of

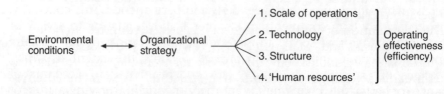

Figure 2.1 Child's model emphasizing the role of strategic choice in influencing structural variation (grossly simplified). *Source*: Child (1972), © British Sociological Association.

strategic choice commences with an evaluation of the organization's position within its environment, the 'congeniality' of its resources and its values and expectations (SWOT analysis in all but name). Goals and objectives are set on the basis of such evaluation which are to be reflected in the strategic actions that follow. Such strategic actions (diversification, retrenchment or product/market development, for example) will then require the (re)deployment or (re)design of internal resources and organization structure so as to 'fit' the chosen strategy. (Readers may compare this model with that implicit in the writings of more recent contributors to strategic management, see the next section.)

A second stage in the model that Child advanced reflects the second consideration pertaining to the notion of structural fit that was outlined above, that is, fit between structural dimensions. The matter of internal consistency among structural dimensions has been seen as critical to the capacity of a particular organizational form to deliver the efficiency or co-ordination required to support the organization's strategy and performance (Chandler, 1962; Galbraith and Kazanjian, 1986). The basic premise is that a change in product/market strategy may require change in all structural dimensions so as to maintain fit with the new strategy (as above) but also that a change in one structural dimension will necessitate a change in the others, again in order to maintain structural fit. The dimensions in question refer to the definition of the tasks that need to be performed within the organization, the allocation of human, financial and technical resources to the performance of those activities and the splitting up and integration of parts of the whole organization so as to facilitate specialization but also co-ordination of work responsibilities, *inter alia*. Underpinning this, of course, is the assumption that organizations with good (and early) fit in these respects will enjoy an advantage over competitors and that organizations that do not attain good fit, or lag behind their rivals in achieving it, will suffer in terms of their internal efficiency and ability to respond to changing external circumstances (Galbraith and Kazanjian, 1986). The relationship suggested between strategy, structural variables and performance on this view is shown in Figure 2.2.

It is worth bearing in mind the comments of Pettigrew and Whipp (1991) regarding the 'dangerous reliance on [structural] fit' when reading both this and the following chapter. The first potential source of danger lies in the extent to which contributions to the debate treat the matching together of structural dimensions and organizational strategy as some once-and-for-all exercise where fit assumes a timelessness and permanence. This concern is mirrored in my own comments in Chapter 1 above, relating to a view of managing change that speaks to issues of flexibility and renewal, and the avoidance of static approaches to change. Second, the extent to which problems of transition and failure are underestimated in accounts of change (or better still 'changing') is another potentially worrying feature of portrayals of fit, as exemplified by the invitation from the literature on corporate excellence to adopt the apparent success formulae of exemplar firms, with the management of cultural change usually near the top of the list.

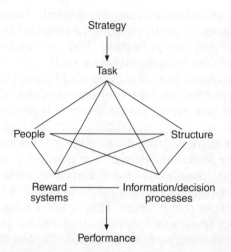

Figure 2.2 An illustration of structural fit among organizational design variables. *Source*: adapted from Galbraith and Kazanjian (1986).

Finally, one other aspect of the dangerous reliance on structural fit is the narrowness of the conception of structure such that network or inter-organizational relationships which might bear on issues of resource efficiency or effectiveness are neglected. This too is a criticism that might be borne in mind over the sections and chapters to follow.

THE POSITIONING/PORTERIAN VIEW OF COMPETITION AND FIT

As mentioned previously, this discussion gives a brief review of the Porterian view of competition and competitive advantage. The contribution of Michael Porter has been to enhance our understanding of the dynamics of industries and competition, albeit in a limited way. For Porter (1980: 3):

> the key aspect of the firm's environment is the industry or industries in which it competes. Industry structure has a strong influence in determining the competitive rules of the game as well as the strategies potentially available to the firm.

Viewed in this way, any development or change of strategy within an organization is governed by prevailing or future industry-level factors. Significantly, the power of these factors in determining the nature of competition and the strategies open to particular organizations is such that Porter's primary framework for analysing industries refers to the 'five *force*' model. The next part of the discussion summarizes the Porterian view of competition with reference to this framework.

Put simply, the merit of the five force framework rests on the insight that its application can generate regarding the attractiveness of an industry in which an organization may be located. Porter defines industry attractiveness in terms of profit potential, where this is measured by long-run return on invested capital (Porter, 1980: 3). Since different industries will be subject to forces which will affect their long-term profit potential differently, the argument goes, it is important to analyse the source, nature and strength of those factors which ultimately determine industry attractiveness. Why? Because industry attractiveness is deemed to be one of two primary determinants of an organization's profitability, the other being the organization's chosen competitive strategy (Porter, 1980; 1985). The key concept in the Porterian view of competition is extended rivalry. In developing the five force framework Porter is at pains to emphasize that the factors that may crucially affect industry attractiveness go well beyond the actions of current competitors. This is not to understate the importance of rivalry between such competitors. After all, this is central to the five force framework both conceptually and diagrammatically (see Figure 2.3). Rather, it is Porter's intention to bring to attention somewhat broader factors than might otherwise be the case; factors which contribute to the nature of rivalry amongst existing competitors and to the extent that an industry is 'attractive'.

In short, attractive industries are ones where there is stable and relatively low intensity of competitive rivalry. This is likely to be the case where the threat of new entrants to the industry is low, for example if the costs of investing in production plants of the scale necessary to make an impact on the market are prohibitive, or if product differentiation is such that the capability to sustain extensive marketing and promotional campaigns is critical. Porter also cites a lack of substitute products or services, and the extent to which the buyers from and suppliers to the producers in an industry enjoy low bargaining power as further indicators of industry attractiveness. Conversely, industries are unattractive where rivalry between existing competitors is intense (in the case of price wars, for example). This

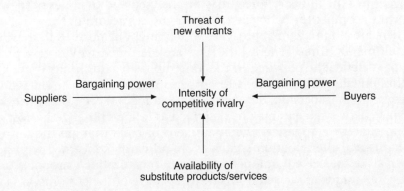

Figure 2.3 Porter's five force framework for analysing industry structure. *Source*: adapted from Porter (1980).

intensity will be exacerbated where the threat of new entrants is high, or substitute products are, or become, widely available and buyers or suppliers are able to exert bargaining power over industry producers.

The effect of intense rivalry is competition which is liable to drive down the level of industry profitability towards the competitive floor rate of return, i.e. that which would be earned in the economist's perfectly competitive industry (Porter, 1980: 5). At these rates, better returns may be won by firms investing in government securities or other better-performing industries. Industries enjoying rates of return higher than those available in capital markets or in other sectors are prone to investment by would-be new entrants (or additional investment by existing rivals). The extent to which new entrants gain a foothold within the industry in question is 'determined' by the strength of the five industry forces quoted above, as is the degree to which new investment serves to drive down rates of return to the competitive floor. And, as Porter puts it, this determines the ability of competitors to sustain 'above-average' returns (Porter, 1980: 6).

To recap, industry attractiveness is one primary determinant of organizational profitability, according to Porter. The other is the competitive strategy that individual organizations pursue. Essentially, the generic strategies framework relates the underlying, fundamental strategic options available at the organizational level. The link with Porter's approach to understanding critical factors operating at the level of the industry sector concerns the way in which organizations are able to defend against the various industry level forces, through their strategic moves. Porter defines competitive strategy as 'taking offensive or defensive actions to create a defendable position in an industry, to cope successfully with the five competitive forces and thereby yield a superior return on investment for the firm' (1980: 34). Moreover, with the purpose of this present chapter firmly in mind, it is important to note that Porter cites the essence of formulating competitive strategy in terms of 'relating a company to its environment', in particular to its industry environment (1980: 3). The firm does have choices however; this is not environmental determinism as discussed above, since the industry forces may be analysed and the rules of the game known to competitors who exercise their choices accordingly.

There are a number of approaches which might be pursued to these ends but ultimately three generic strategies are identified which may provide such a 'defendable' position, in the long run, as regards industry forces, as well as enabling organizations to outperform competitors in an industry. These are cost leadership, differentiation and focus (Porter, 1980; 1985).

The generic strategies may be described as follows. Briefly, the cost leadership strategy emphasizes the attainment of costs that are the lowest in an industry. Differentiation strategies are primarily concerned with building 'real' or 'perceived' uniqueness into an organization's products or services (i.e. unique as viewed from the perspective of the customer). As such differentiation may be pursued on the basis of the innovation of tangible products or through marketing activity aimed at enhancing the image of a product as 'exclusive' in some way. Where cost leadership is predicated upon the achievement of lowest costs, with the implication of lowest pricing (though not a point that is made explicit by Porter), a differentiation strategy is typically associated with premium pricing. The third generic strategy is focus. This strategy combines a choice of the other two generic strategies described above with the serving of a narrow, rather than a broad, strategic target market. Hence the scope of activities here is restricted and the central aim is to serve well either specific buyer groups, or geographical markets, for example.

Although Porter is careful to state that these generic strategies are not mutually exclusive, he does (rather infamously) warn of the dangers of not selecting a clear, consistent and unambiguous generic strategy and, further, of the perils of *mixing* generic strategies. This is where Porter's 'stuck in the middle' thesis has achieved some notoriety. For newcomers to the topic of managing change it may not be transparent how this issue connects to the theme of this book, but its relevance should become clearer over the next few paragraphs.

The central argument that Porter advances is that:

> The three generic strategies are alternative viable approaches to dealing with the competitive forces ... the firm failing to develop its strategy in at least one of the three directions – a firm that is 'stuck in the middle' – is in an extremely poor strategic situation ... The firm stuck in the middle is almost guaranteed low profitability. It either loses high-volume customers who demand low prices or must bid away its profits to get this business away from low-cost firms. Yet it also loses high-margin businesses ... to the firms who are focused on high-margin targets or have achieved differentiation overall.
>
> *(Porter, 1980: 39–42)*

The capabilities required to support the generic strategy to be selected provide some explanation for the Porterian approach. Thus the pursuit of a mix of cost leadership and differentiation generic strategies would invite failure since the implementation of such strategies: 'usually requires total commitment and supporting organizational arrangements that are diluted if there is more than one primary target' (Porter, 1980: 35). Moreover, an organization that is stuck in the middle will, according to Porter, be likely to suffer from a confused corporate culture and, in addition, operational policies that are inconsistent with the chosen strategy(ies). This malaise is compounded for firms in difficulty by a tendency to switch continually between generic strategies, which, owing to their incompatible resource and managerial requirements, is a tendency that is 'almost always doomed to failure' (Porter, 1980: 42).

A number of bones of contention arise from Porter's prescriptions which relate to the primary themes of this book, such as the view taken of the relationship between strategy and structure and the general treatment of the concept of strategic fit and the means by which fit between the resources and environment of an organization may be obtained. (In addition, there are several other specific conceptual and practical limitations and criticisms that have been made of aspects of the Porterian approach that readers may follow up elsewhere, for example in Faulkner and Johnson, 1992). One way of addressing these is to begin by considering the skills and organizational requirements that Porter defines as necessary for the pursuit of the generic strategies that he identifies. These strategies suggest alternative organizational forms and structural mechanisms that need to be implemented in order for the selected generic strategy to be effective. In the case of competing on the basis of a cost leadership strategy this is a matter of installing tightly defined cost control and reporting procedures, incentives based on meeting strict quantifiable targets and 'intense supervision' of employees. However, for the pursuit of differentiation the scene is rather of an organization characterized by the need for cross-functional co-ordination (i.e. across the whole value chain in Porterian terms), an emphasis on the creativity, skills and expertise of employees plus reliance on qualitative measures regarding incentives. In a throwaway line, Porter states that the pursuit of alternative generic strategies may also require different styles of leadership and may 'translate into very different corporate cultures and atmospheres' (1980: 41). Fundamentally, this is a functionalist view of the strategy–structure relationship that bears the hallmarks of the classical approach to managing strategy and change. It is an approach that is, apparently, amenable to planning and analysis. First, one analyses industry attractiveness and the dynamics of competition. Then one considers where, on the basis of the foregoing analysis, the organization should be positioned within the industry, leading to a choice of generic strategy. And then, finally, once this matter of strategic choice has been decided, implementation centring upon the required skills, resources and organizational design issues ensues. In this way, implementation or execution is separated from the activity of choice and the consideration of issues pertaining to structural questions follows the taking of decisions related to the organization's corporate and competitive strategy. Moreover, this approach neglects issues relating to the possibility of internal dissent and politics which would feature in a processual or interpretive perspective and although certain aspects of the external context of organizations are brought into play (i.e. industry related), others such as the influence of governmental policies or other institutional factors are lacking. So, whilst changing generic strategies is, admittedly, considered by Porter to be a painful exercise, the Porterian approach is to dissuade organizations from attempting change, rather than to account for the stresses and processes involved in managing organizational transformation in practice. This is reflected in the stricture to sustain commitment to one of the generic strategies so as to avoid getting 'stuck in the middle' and the relative lack of attention to the exploration of why, according to Porter (1980: 42), firms in difficulty tend to 'flip back and forth over time among the generic strategies' and issues of change that might be associated with any such tendency.

SUMMARY

A brief reiteration of the principal criticisms of the positioning approach in terms of its relevance to understanding the management of organizational change may now be given. First, the preoccupation with industry- or organizational-level affairs serves to neglect or to undervalue important contextual factors which may impinge on competition, competitiveness and strategic change, for example those connected to wider governmental, institutional and socio-cultural considerations. Second, and linked to the first point, both industry-level factors as well as broader macro-environmental trends, in so far as they are taken into account, are assumed to represent some 'objective' environment external to the organization. Third, and again related to the previous point, this treatment of external environmental analysis as amenable to objective, quantifiable analysis, is underpinned by assumptions informed by the much criticized classical, rational approach to decision-making. Fourth, processes of strategy formulation and change tend to emphasize the role and discretion of individual, entrepreneurial leaders or, at least, the senior management élite, yet understate organization-wide influences on strategic objectives and the course of strategy implementation in practice. And finally, in addition to the point made above concerning ignorance of contextual aspects of strategic development and change, it is notable how the ebb and flow of the dynamics of competition and organizational behaviour over time tend to be neglected in much of the strategy literature that is of the Porterian variety. As the following chapter will show, some of these criticisms also apply to treatments of concepts of fit and organizational change identified with proponents of excellence thinking.

CAPABILITIES, EXCELLENCE AND STRUCTURAL FIT $\boxed{3}$

INTRODUCTION

The essence of this chapter of the book is the discussion of the relevance of notions of structural fit and commitment to understanding strategic management and change. In a simplistic way the staple diet of much business school teaching on strategy, for which the ingredients include PEST and SWOT analysis, gives some indication of avenues for achieving strategic fit. Chapter 2 exposed some general limitations of such fare. Thus one danger of such approaches is that students or practitioners become obsessed with lists of the supposedly objective factors that are identified as possibly constraining or promoting alternative strategic options. A second possible deficiency is that external environmental factors are treated as being 'out there', rather than reflecting the interactions of diverse actors, including those within the firm under scrutiny. Third, the one-off nature of the model of strategy embodied in this type of thinking detracts from a more holistic and ongoing view of the various external factors, the interaction of different parties at organizational, industrial and macro-environmental levels, and the implications for organizational change or inertia that interpretations of external environmental events and signals may suggest. Whilst there is no pretence to exhaustiveness here, the aim of what follows in this chapter is to take the discussion of structural fit on from the previous chapter to address the foibles of some commonly advanced arguments regarding the nature and sources of organizational excellence. This entails consideration of a collection of approaches which together comprise a resource- or capabilities-based view of strategy, or which constitute contributions to the excellence literature or the 'culture industry'. Despite the air of contentiousness that surrounds the debate between proponents of these views and those working within the tradition of the positioning school, they share common ground, operating within a voluntarist framework. As the previous chapter did with strategic fit to the fore, the following sections will illustrate this point with regard to the manipulation of organizational structure and culture and the notion of structural fit.

THE SIGNIFICANCE OF ORGANIZATIONAL CAPABILITIES

In contrast to the positioning school, a view that has emerged in recent years emphasizes the development of superior organizational capabilities in accounting for strategies that may confer competitive advantage. A 'good' strategy is one by which an organization can build and sustain distinctive skills and abilities in terms of the management of its internal resources and, if successful, such a strategy allows that organization to redefine the basis of competition within its sector. Hence, taking this view, organizations may well be able to alter aspects of industry structure and competition (i.e. mould the competitive environment to the organization's favour) rather more than is the case with the positioning school where, essentially, organizations have to choose strategies in order to achieve fit with conditions in the external environment. This does not mean that issues of 'fit' do not feature prominently in the writings of proponents of the resource-based view. Rather, the general approach is at odds with those according to the positioning approach on the matter of the relative significance of external and internal factors to the strategy and performance of organizations.

The resource-based perspective is exemplified by those who consider a number of variations on much the same theme, relating to the strategic significance of managing resources, capabilities, competence (or 'competencies') and so on. In origin, this view owes much to the influence of those who offer a critique of the neoclassical approach to conceptualizing and understanding competition (e.g. Nelson and Winter, 1982; Schumpeter, 1911) or who identified new bases of competition and organization that were emerging in the 1970s and 1980s (Abernathy, 1978; Abernathy *et al.*, 1981; Hayes and Abernathy, 1980; Hayes and Wheelwright, 1984). Whether the protagonists refer to a notion of 'resources', 'capabilities' or 'competence/competency', the concerns and underlying message are common.

The cornerstone of the approach is that the performance of an organization is governed by the resources that it possesses, develops and co-ordinates. It is the quality of the management of such resources and the translation of these into competencies or capabilities that separates the better from the poorer performers in a sector. An important facet of this view concerns the relevance of both tangible and intangible resources to the enhancement of strategic capability. In particular, the role of technology and knowledge management in developing and sustaining competitiveness is receiving increasing attention in the strategy and change literatures. In addition, the connection between the building of strategically relevant capabilities and the operational procedures and rules of thumb that govern everyday actions within organizations is also being recognized. An essential point to make in a book such as this is that one should not assume any existing commitment within an organization to competition on the basis of capabilities or competencies, nor the permanence of such distinctive capabilities that are built. The latter may well be temporary due to imitation by rivals, for example, or loss of key internal personnel. With this in mind the upgrading or rebuilding of capabilities may be seen in terms of the reorientation of existing organizational routines. Routines may be said to govern the manner in which individuals and groups in organizations habitually perform their work (Nelson and Winter, 1982). Hence the breaking down of 'outmoded' routines and the development of new practices represents one of the key tasks facing those involved in effecting strategic renewal through ongoing attention to capabilities and resource management. This latter point brings to mind the essence of literature on the subject of organizational learning which will be addressed more directly in Chapter 4, below. For now, it is merely the extent to which organizational learning is cast in terms of the acquisition of knowledge and its application to functional and cross-functional organizational skills and strategic capabilities that needs to be noted.

Contributions to this resource-based perspective differ in the degree to which they focus upon:

- the relevance of product or process technology to achieving sustainable competitive advantage, where 'technology' tends to be conceived of in terms of its 'hardware' or 'technique' senses
- issues of change pertinent to organizing for such a basis of competition, including structural and values-related aspects of product innovation or the implementation of process innovations.

Prahalad and Hamel's (1990) work on what they term 'core competencies' is essentially of the former variety, being primarily (though not entirely) concerned with identifying underlying sources of competitiveness. Prahalad and Hamel make a distinction between organizations conceiving themselves in terms of a portfolio of business units and those which are defined in terms of a portfolio of competencies. Where the former of these stances corresponds to traditional positioning approaches wherein strategic business units in a portfolio target positions within defined markets segments and resource allocation is made on the basis of these units' individual performance, the core competencies approach is somewhat different. Here, the synergies between business units are conceived on the basis of underlying organization-wide abilities and knowledge and their co-ordination. Thus taking this view competitiveness:

> derives from an ability to build, at lower cost and more speedily than competitors, the core competencies that spawn unanticipated products. The real sources of advantage are to be found in management's ability to consolidate corporate wide technologies and production skills into competencies that empower individual businesses to adapt quickly to changing opportunities.
>
> *(Prahalad and Hamel, 1990: 81)*

Key to an appreciation of the strategic implications of core competencies is the manner in which these may translate into core products and ultimately end products. The example of Vickers and their supply of control systems to various markets including aerospace, automotive and defence sectors illustrates the argument. At Vickers, core competencies comprised the design and development of electronic, electrical and mechanical controls and components. Core products that resulted from the application of such competencies include electronic sensors, electric generators and fans, whilst end products took the form of complete control systems packages, components, servicing or user training (Prahalad and Hamel, 1990).

The hallmark of success in organizations such as Vickers, but also NEC, Sony and CNN, is only partly explained with reference to their attention to core competencies and the implications that these may have for accelerated and profuse product innovation. In addition, it is argued, a reconsideration of the traditional notion of strategic fit is warranted. Hence it is suggested that the preoccupation with fit that has dominated strategic thinking over the years should be supplanted, or at the very least balanced, with a frame of thought that considers strategy in terms of 'stretch' (Hamel and Prahalad, 1993). This notion of stretch moves beyond the role of resources conferring competitiveness, it is claimed. What now is to assume primacy is the *misfit* between resources and aspirations. The essential message is that organizations lacking ambition and vision may be vulnerable, even though they may enjoy a surfeit of resources at their disposal compared to those organizations with 'stretched' aspirations and a creative approach to leveraging what resources they do have. Prahalad and Hamel are at pains to disclaim a raw 'small is beautiful' philosophy. This matter of leveraging resources in the management of stretch does not, they say, necessarily entail the pursuit of downsizing in the hope of becoming 'lean and mean'. Instead, the variety of means by which resources may be leveraged include the concentration of their allocation on an organization's key strategic theme or mission, their more efficient accumulation, as in the case of the acquisition of technological know-how through cross-border alliances or licensing.

Similar fundamental concerns are to be found in a related approach which focuses upon the nature of competition based on organizational capabilities (Stalk *et al.*, 1992). The success of capabilities-based competitors is ascribed to their ability to leverage resources in the quest to translate key business processes into products which provide superior customer value. Again, in contrast to the received view, the manner of resource allocation required to fulfil this notion of competitive strategy demands a holistic approach, rather than one based upon the portfolio concept of evaluating and investing in individual strategic business units. According to Stalk *et al.*, the essential difference between competency- and capabilities-based competition, is that the former emphasizes individual technologies and production skills whereas the latter considers intangible, less obvious aspects of competitiveness. Thus, whilst Prahalad and Hamel portray the myriad products (motorcycles, cars and lawnmowers) that stem from Honda's technical competencies residing in engine design and manufacture, Stalk *et al.* exemplify the additional insight they claim for their approach with reference to Honda's attention to dealer training and support – a capability complementary to their aforementioned competencies (Stalk *et al.*, 1992).

A variant of this view has been expounded by those who seek to go more explicitly into the role of organizational values and norms in conferring what have been referred to as 'core capabilities' (Leonard-Barton, 1992). On this view, it is argued, the interaction of such values and norms with the knowledge-base and technical and managerial systems of an organization needs to be emphasized if our understanding of the management of organizational capability is to be improved. Further, the relevance of the use of language and, more specifically, the employment of metaphor and analogy, in triggering the knowledge-creation process and contributing to the building of organization-wide product development capability has been analysed (Nonaka, 1991).

As far as the management of change is concerned, it is recognized that managers within individual organizations will have pre-existing orientations towards issues of strategy and the performance of operational activities. Hence the 'challenge' of becoming a capabilities-based competitor may well necessitate a transformation of perception regarding the definition of processes as the source of competitiveness and ways in which an organization might be reshaped to facilitate competition on this basis. Case study 3.1 – Medequip – is offered as illumination of the manner in which processes of change occurring in one organization moving towards being a capabilities-based competitor are analysed (Stalk *et al.*, 1992). As the reader may note, there are certain similarities of orientation between this account of change and the traditional way of accounting for change discussed above, notwithstanding the claim that is made of a new approach to conceptualizing sources of competitiveness. A number of remarks may be made in this regard. First, the case study is of the episodic variety complained of above. As well as the clear lack of the longitudinal dimension required to portray the ebb and flow of strategies and changes at Medequip over time, the 'structure follows strategy' thesis appears still to be very much alive and kicking. Thus first comes the strategy as reflected in the move towards competing on capabilities, then follows the adaptation of organizational structure with the creation of 'cells' and attention to some issues of structural fit through the development of employee training and reward systems so that staff are motivated and able to perform their new roles. Moreover, the process of change is avowedly top-down and the leading role is played by the chief executive officer (compare this to the accounts of collectively led and operationally driven change contained in Pettigrew and Whipp [1991] for example). Finally, the account centres on the internal aspects of change at Medequip; there is little that is connected to understanding the industry context, never mind wider economic or regulatory considerations, yet at the same time there is no reference to any more symbolic or internal political issues that might have affected the change process.

**CASE STUDY
3.1**

Medequip

The essence of this case concerns Medequip, a pseudonym for a manufacturer of medical equipment, and the process by which, according to Stalk *et al.*, it became a 'capabilities-based' competitor. The change process was triggered by the need to regain market share that had been lost to a new competitor, which had introduced a lower-priced, lower-quality version of Medequip's most successful product. Medequip's response at first was to introduce a new product to rival that of the new entrant but, on further investigation, the firm's managers came to define the problem confronting them in terms of Medequip's business processes, rather than individual products and markets. A key aspect of developing the capabilities-based strategy turned on the recognition that an important source of value for Medequip was the informal link-up that had developed between its sales function and its on-site service personnel, where the latter had been placed at accounts full-time. The company decided to more explicitly integrate the above functions into a combined sales-service (and also order-entry) capability, guaranteeing on-site service to targeted accounts (basically those which were not already dominated by a single rival). The benefits of these moves included the freeing up of the time of sales staff who could concentrate on generating long-term business and the training of service personnel which allowed them to generate new sales leads. Market share increased by almost 50 per cent and profit levels rose.

Stalk *et al.* account for the changes referred to above with reference to four key steps by which Medequip are said to have developed the new capabilities-based strategy:

1. Shifting the strategic framework to achieve aggressive goals – i.e. Medequip's abandonment of their traditional product/market orientation.

2. Organizing around the chosen capability and ensuring that employees have the necessary skills and resources to achieve it – for example, the restructuring of sales and service functions, the training of service reps in sales techniques and also the support of information systems in enabling service staff to access data about the company's product line, all in fulfilment of Medequip's strategy (cf. 'structure follows strategy' thesis).

3. Making progress visible and bringing its measurement and reward into alignment – note this version of structural fit in action. At Medequip, new measures needed to be developed relating to the contribution of individual customers to profitability, on the basis of which service teams were recompensed, again in support of the company's competitive strategy.

4. Not delegate the leadership of the transformation – since capabilities are cross-functional and change towards competing on this basis painful, the process is not one which can be left to middle managers, it is argued. Indeed, the hands-on guidance of the CEO, who oversees the whole process is required. Although the active involvement of top-line managers is recognized, it is the CEO who evaluates any proposals and makes the final decision. Not a particularly collective view of the leadership of change.

Source: based on Stalk *et al.* (1992).

ORGANIZATIONAL CULTURE AND 'EXCELLENCE THINKING'

A few paragraphs are due on one other pervasive strain of thinking that has been the subject of much debate within the field of strategic management and change. This concerns what has been referred to as the cottage industry relating to the literature on 'excellence'. The case for the defence has been put in many volumes by writers such as Tom Peters. The basic claim is that companies enjoying superior performance are characterized by strong cultures and structural mechanisms which promote entrepreneurialism, innovation and attention to customer needs. 'Excellence' has been defined in terms of the continuous innovative capacity of the large companies that featured in the Peters and Waterman research. The performance of such organizations has been explained with reference to the extraordinary commitment of 'ordinary' employees and the translation of their efforts into sustained, exceptional financial performance. Further, a number of large so-called 'top-performing' companies (e.g. IBM, 3M and Proctor and Gamble) have been cited for their attention to the building of new organizational capabilities related to product innovation, employee relations and so forth (Peters and Waterman, 1982).

In Search Of Excellence developed a diagnostic framework for organizational analysis as well as specific criteria for success, which are reiterated in Tom Peters's subsequent volumes, videos, and so on, as well as in the work of other disciples of excellence. The limitations that Peters and Waterman perceived of the strategy–structure debate as it was being addressed prior to the publication of *In Search Of Excellence* led them to offer the McKinsey 7-S framework, which is suggested as a useful way of thinking about the style, systems, skills, staffing and shared values of organizations, in addition to matters of strategy and structure. Moving from diagnosis to the issue of prescriptive remedies for organizational malaise, Peters and Waterman offered a number of now famous practical suggestions stemming from their analysis of the attributes of the excellent companies that they researched (Peters and Waterman, 1982: 13–16). (Note that the authors of *In Search Of Excellence* were very much less concerned with sources of malaise in organizations and the causes of poor performance than with the secrets of successful companies, an orientation which is reflected in their somewhat skewed research sample). These eight attributes emphasized:

- a bias for action
- closeness to customers
- autonomy and entrepreneurship
- productivity through people
- the centrality of organizational philosophy and values and a hands-on approach to managing
- sticking to the knitting (i.e. what the organization is best at doing)
- simple form, lean staff
- simultaneous loose-tight properties (i.e. managing the paradox of decentralized decision-making and strong core organizational values).

These attributes reflect a wider preoccupation with three central themes common to 'post-*Excellence*' thinking. These concern aspects of organizational culture and their relevance to employee commitment and receptivity to change; the merits of alternative structural forms and mechanisms for promoting employee autonomy and empowerment whilst providing for heightened market sensitivity and organizational efficiency; and the nature of competitive advantage, linked to the definition of organizational boundaries in excellent organizations and to the competitive strategies that they pursue.

As noted above, at the core of the excellence viewpoint is the argument that the attitudes and values of individual employees are key to the building of organizational cultures capable of continuous innovation and receptivity to change. Thus 'them and us' labour relations are 'out' and engendering individual commitment to core organizational values is 'in' and all-important. If one delves into *In Search of Excellence* in this connection, one finds the philosophy of IBM, for example, being quoted in terms of 'respect for the individual' and commitment to core values in another 'excellent' company, 3M, cited as being analogous to the conformity of brainwashed members of an extreme religious sect to its central beliefs (Peters and Waterman, 1982). Case study 3.2 captures the excellence of IBM as related by Peters and Waterman.

In terms of issues of structural form and organizational design, the prescription for excellence is clear: decentralize! Reduce hierarchy! Encourage (cross-functional) team-building! The argument tends to proceed along these now familiar lines. First, (and somewhat unsurprisingly) issues of structural form cannot, and should not, be considered in isolation from 'people' issues. As Peters put it: 'There is no such thing as a good structural answer apart from people considerations and vice versa' (Peters and Waterman, 1982: 9).

Kanter expresses the point in terms of one of the key principles underpinning the 'thoughtful' restructuring of 'giant' organizations in the US during the 1980s: 'The principle is clear: Staffs are no longer considered

IBM 'A': a model of excellence CASE STUDY 3.2

IBM is cited again and again as an exemplary organization in *In Search of Excellence*. One of the key aspects of the organization's success until the mid-1980s has been cited as its respect for its employees, which the main text of this chapter has already discussed. Another is the ideology and values of the firm. Here, Peters and Waterman quote the statement 'IBM means service' as one which 'underscores the company's overpowering devotion to the individual customer' but also a statement of core values which provided a degree of latitude for employees. Thus within that general mission, everyone from the very bottom up was 'prodded' to think and act in whatever way was appropriate to attend to the needs of individual customers. This ability to manage this paradox of strong central values and individual action-orientated autonomy is cited as vital to underpinning IBM's service obsession such that the latter 'became almost a reflex in IBM ... with no chinks in the (service and closeness to the customer) armour'.

Source: Adapted from Peters and Waterman (1982: 159, 160).

'overhead' but potential sources of value; they are not watchdogs and interveners but suppliers serving customers' (Kanter, 1989: 98). This principle Kanter contrasts with 'mindless' downsizing wherein the focus is only on the 'less' of the doing more with less imperative. Here, the view of employees is primarily as costs rather than as assets and organizations adopting such an approach are blind to the value in terms of the skills and experience that resides with employees which leaves that organization when the redundancy notices of such staff take effect (Kanter, 1989: 89).

Second, while cognizant of the danger implicit in over-focusing on issues of structural form, the excellence approach contends that certain structural arrangements do little to foster employee autonomy, creativity and commitment whilst others do, with dramatic implications for organizational performance. The work of Kanter is again recalled here, particularly in view of her definition of segmentalist and integrative organizations. Essentially, the segmentalist organization is characterized by centralized decision-making, an 'elevator mentality' and the retreat of staff to the territory of their 'home' department. On the other hand, integrative organizations are characterized by devolved decision-making, facilitated by freer access to organizational resources and mechanisms to foster and support cross-functional, lateral co-ordination in the organization (Kanter, 1989). The latter type of organization, consequently, is considered to be appropriate for the innovation and flexibility demanded by new patterns of demand and competition. It is in this way that fit between environment and organization is said to be best effected in practice.

In certain quarters the message regarding the appropriateness of alternative structural forms is quite evangelical. Peters, for instance, is able to advocate that no more than five hierarchical reporting levels should exist in any organization. He instructs that:

> No more than five layers of management are necessary, regardless of firm size; limit layers in any facility to three at the most. Get staffs out into the field and encourage them to be 'business team members' rather than narrow functional specialists … Minimum spans of control at the front line should be one supervisor for every 25 to 75 nonsupervisors.
>
> *(Peters, 1989: 354)*.

Similarly, though less stridently, Quinn quotes examples such as Federal Express, where the number of hierarchical layers between the chief executive officer and non-managerial employees was reduced to five (see Chapter 7 in this volume), and Union Pacific where six layers of hierarchy were removed (Quinn, 1992).

The analysis and recommendations that have been discussed above with regard to structural choices tend to imply the pursuit of certain corporate or competitive strategies. Here, 'stick to the knitting' remains surely one of the best known and pervasive axioms ever to have emanated from the field of management. The basic message is 'don't leave home base' – excellence rarely comes from straying from the business or activity that an organization has got to know well. Moreover, this is a prescription that contrasts starkly with calls to avoid putting one's eggs into one basket by means of diversifying the organization's portfolio so as to reduce potential risks (cf. Ansoff, 1965). Further, the advice about the knitting applies to large corporations as well to smaller entities. Essentially, it is a view that in Porter's terms advocates (differentiation) focus and a restricted definition of organizational activities that has much in sympathy with the resource-based perspective of corporate and competitive strategy.

Explaining the basis of her position, Kanter puts it thus: 'the *corporation-as-department-store*, a gigantic entity with every conceivable aspect of the production chain and every service it uses under its own roof, is being replaced by the *corporation-as-boutique*. *Focus* is the key word' (Kanter, 1989: 97, original italics). However, the principal concern of writers from the resource or excellence approaches is with the structural and operational sources of competitiveness and adaptation to market changes.

There are a number of pitfalls that need to be identified regarding the notion of structural fit that is invoked, whether explicitly or implicitly, by those who are associated with the excellence or resource-based strands of the strategy literature. (The reader will observe that in certain respects these criticisms bear some resemblance to those applied above to the notion of strategic fit and positioning-related approaches.)

At the heart of the matter is the degree to which any link between organizational structure, cultural change and ensuing improvements in strategic performance is oversimplified, misunderstood or deemed amenable to a 'planned' approach. As Wilson (1992) puts it, the assumption that structural form can produce required types of culture and behaviour is a normative claim that is typical of the excellence literature. This strain of thinking adopts a 'structuralist' view of organizational culture and change. The principal sins that are committed here are both theoretical and empirical in nature. For example, one may criticize the assumption that only one structural form will 'fit all', that is the lean, decentralized organization becomes 'the one best way' to organize. Moreover, to adopt this structural form is viewed as representing the means by which the culture of an organization may be remoulded, in the bid to facilitate the customer-responsiveness and entrepreneurship of its employees. Furthermore, the whole business of structural and cultural change is presented usually as the strategic choice of the heroic chief executive and/or an evidently 'plannable' exercise, in a manner similar to that associated with strategic development as addressed from the positioning perspective. Of course, evidence of strategic change in practice readily underlines these limitations. It is now well known that certain of the companies featuring in *In Search of Excellence* have found their much-touted success difficult to sustain, necessitating quite painful change. The Icarus paradox is an interesting notion to introduce at this stage, concerned as it is with the idea that a 'strong' culture (however one defines this) may be an indicator of failing rather than succeeding performance. The case of IBM is especially noteworthy in this respect (see Case study 3.3). Finally, it just may be possible that there are other explanations than those to do with structural form or type of organizational culture which may be invoked to better understand why organizations perform well or badly at particular points in time, or more interestingly, why this performance tends to vary over time and in relation to that of others within the same sector or of similar size. Perhaps the organization enjoyed a monopoly position which was eroded by new industry developments (IBM again); or maybe the organization relied upon government funding which was then withdrawn (just one of the factors used to explain both downturns and turnarounds in British car firms in the 1970s and 1980s). Basically, organizational structure is just one part of the story of the change and a more modest view of voluntaristic choice needs to be adopted.

IBM 'B' and the Icarus paradox   **CASE STUDY 3.3**

Whereas the IBM 'A' case study illustrated Peters and Waterman's view of that organization as one of their exemplars of excellence, Danny Miller's book tells a different tale not too many years later. As such it offers a cautionary tale about the temporal nature of organizational performance and the need to consider the change process as it unravels through time, rather than in episodic snapshots.

In the Icarus paradox, IBM 'post-excellence' history may be seen in terms of what Miller refers to as the 'decoupling trajectory'. This is where the strengths that helped to build organizational success on the basis of its sales abilities subsequently become part of the reason for that organization's decline. For IBM, the roots of their spectacular 1980s losses were considered to stem from the following two sources:

1. Product-line proliferation. IBM brought out too many marginal lines which competed with each other, rather than bringing out significant new products that could make a difference. Moreover, in the early 1980s, gaps were left 'in the growing workstation business and in software for networking computers'.
2. Insular decision-making. Miller considers that by 1985 'even IBM, the legendary listener was ... losing some of its former edge'. It had lost touch with its customers and was now persisting in 'trying to sell them products when what they wanted was solutions' (i.e. in getting their computers to talk to each other). Part of the trouble was that IBM had become so successful that 'selling became a breeze', where on the way up the company's sales reps were 'obsessed' with the customer, they now were spending only one-third of their time with customers, such was their complacency.

Source: Adapted from Miller (1992: 169–70).

SUMMARY

Although the distinction has been made between views of strategy in terms of their association with 'positioning' and 'resource-based' perspectives to the subject of strategic management, they do have something in common as summed up by Pettigrew and Whipp's (1991: 240) reference to the 'dangerous reliance on fit'. The sections above have shown the relevance of notions of fit to an illumination of the conduct of strategy in organizations. However, it has also been shown that some care is warranted where the application of concepts of strategic and structural fit to voluntaristic, or overly deterministic, understanding of managing change is concerned. Developing a soft determinist/weak voluntarist middle ground between the aforementioned perspectives might be achieved in the following manner. First, by addressing practical implications for change of bounded rationality and organizational politics in an updated version of incrementalism that emphasizes aspects (and problems of) flexibility, learning and knowledge. Second, by recognizing the role of cognition and managerial judgement in interpreting environmental data and in perceiving the mission of the organization and its standing within its industry sector, thus indicating the relevance of an interpretive view of possibilities and difficulties of change. Third, a variety of 'institutional' approaches help to shed light on the complex of doing, learning, context and change in organizations. All of the preceding considerations are taken up in the following chapter.

FLEXIBILITY-RELATED, INSTITUTIONAL AND INTERPRETIVE EXPLANATIONS OF CHANGE 4

INTRODUCTION

The previous two chapters have been concerned with orthodox views of strategic change. While areas of dispute exist between 'positioning' and 'capabilities/excellence' approaches to understanding strategy and change, the common ground between these views has been identified. In particular, attention has been drawn to some of the limitations which apply to such views which emphasize strategic or structural fit. This chapter aims to deepen an understanding of these approaches to change. However, the intention is to provide some means by which the reader will be enabled to move beyond conventional strategic management to consider insights into the process and implementation of change which may be drawn from less popular approaches to the subject. In terms of more clearly understanding the literature which focuses upon either strategy–environmental fit or the structure–culture–strategy relationship, notions of flexibility will be of help, especially if their discussion is allied to some notion of a knowledge-creating, or 'learning' organization (see the following section). An interesting and valuable departure in the middle of the chapter takes the reader into areas of 'institutional theory'. Aspects of this further our appreciation of organizational restructuring. However, in some respects the introduction of an institutional viewpoint has more to do with the material presented towards the end of this chapter. Here, the primary concern is with more political, behavioural and symbolic explanations of change. With these in mind, the importance of individual interpretations of the legitimacy of change and employee commitment (or non-commitment) to its implementation comes to the fore.

In general, the chapter takes a turn away from the decisiveness and deliberation of voluntarism in favour of a more messy version of change where organizational adaptation and learning is achieved fitfully, uneasily and is the expression of happenstance, values and power relationships, rather than 'good planning'.

FLEXIBILITY, KNOWLEDGE AND LEARNING

It is necessary to outline what is meant here by 'flexibility'. As it applies to strategy and change, and in a decision-making sense, flexibility may be thought of, initially, in two distinct ways related to: a) adaptability; and b) renewal. Essentially, adaptability represents a static, tactical view of flexibility. This implies a one-off and once-and-for-all adjustment to a changed environment. Renewal is a notion which better captures flexibility in an ongoing sense (Genus, 1995). Hence, strategic renewal is a process of never-ending change which organizations need to undergo in order to remain viable. This renewal concerns an organization's capability to constantly improve the fit between its strategy and external environmental demands and between strategy and internal structure and resources (Huff *et al.*, 1992). The latter sense of flexibility may be seen, therefore, as having a more dynamic orientation to it than the former and 'fit', on this occasion, is a quality that is constantly striven for rather than the one-off quest that is apparent in conventional treatments discussed in the previous two chapters. Hence it is possible to consider much of the orthodox view of change in the light of the 'adaptability' version of flexibility.

There are two aspects of flexibility that need to be considered relevant to the issues central to this volume. These pertain to: a) flexibility within organizations, and b) flexible relations between organizations (Starkey *et al.*, 1991). Arguably, the dominant occupation of the research and literature on strategic change has concerned the first of these, addressing internal, organizational restructuring and culture management, within a contingency-theory based view of organizational design, or at least a severe reading of that literature (see Clark and Staunton [1993], on the misreading of some of the work of Woodward). As the previous chapter showed, the relationship between alternative organizational structures, culture and the development of the customer-responsiveness of employees form central concerns connected to this aspect of flexibility.

Central to such thinking has been the idea of the retreat by large corporations to their core activities (i.e. 'sticking to the knitting'), the development of the core/periphery workforce, and organizational redesign to permit greater knowledge of and sensitivity to market requirements. The appeal (and indeed the rhetoric of the flexible organization) is beguiling and pervasive, partly and perhaps implicitly because of an underlying acceptance of the benefits of a flexible approach to decision-making. However, whilst the work of advocates such as J.B. Quinn (1992) should be acknowledged, there is an abundance of rather sceptical literature on the extent to which organizational restructuring in practice, rather than concept, has been concerned with the adoption of flexible structures in pursuit of strategic benefits. This has been exemplified by the question posed by the title of *Farewell to Flexibility?* (Pollert, 1991). This critical stance is more closely identified with the industrial relations/human resource management literature than strategic management and it will be interesting to compare the treatments of the prescription and practice of restructuring from within the two disciplines in a later chapter (Chapter 7).

Flexible relations between organizations is an issue which has suffered by comparison to the focus on intra-organizational change. However, the matter of contextual relationships between competitors within an industry, with suppliers but also governmental or research organizations, for example, is receiving greater recognition. Interestingly, one of the contributions of Michael Porter's early work (on industry analysis through the five force model) was to emphasize that a wider view of industry competition and dynamics needed to be taken than was then conventional. One of Porter's colleagues, Kathryn Harrigan (1985) has addressed the nature of strategic flexibility, focusing upon aspects of industry structure (such as the resale market for capital equipment) which smooth or impede exit from declining industries. To a lesser extent she also identified managers' psychological commitment to existing strategies as a potential barrier to flexibility, a matter which will be taken up again towards the end of the current chapter. More recently, topics of concern have included the benefits and management of strategic alliances, outsourcing and collaborative relationships with suppliers, while the debate about the merits of the flexible specialization thesis (Piore and Sabel, 1984) have continued to rumble on. Key to both of these aspects of flexibility may be the development of knowledge and learning, either within specific organizations or among networks of firms and other organizations.

At this juncture it is worthwhile to devote some more detailed attention to the subjects of organizational learning and knowledge. To begin with, one notes the distinction between individual learning, individual learning within organizational settings and organizational learning. At the individual level, learning is characterized by changes in the memory content of individuals, which may occur within organizational settings or not. Organizational learning, however, represents changes in organizational memory content which are independent of individuals within the organization (Borum, 1990).

Levitt and March (1988) refer to the various ways in which organizations develop routines that enable recurring activities to be performed without recourse to time-consuming or costly learning processes (where such routines represent the 'encoding' of past experience and thus, in effect, the organizational memory content referred to above). To some extent these involve the imitation or diffusion of 'best practice' from elsewhere, a process which is addressed by various types of institutional theory (see the following section) and is exemplified by the popularity of 'Japanese' organizational innovations over recent years. They may also involve the recruitment of new staff who possess the competences that an organization needs (i.e. routines are acquired). An interesting point here concerns the extent to which organizations are able to 'appropriate' such individual knowledge (cf. Teece, 1987). In Levitt and March's view organizational learning through such acquisitive means runs the risk of leaving organizations vulnerable to individual 'expert' employees, hence their conception of organizational routines avoiding overreliance on such staff.

This is somewhat different in orientation from another view of organizational routines associated with March, from that taken in previous work of his. Cyert and March's (1963) notion of routines needs to be thought of in the context of their explanation of why organizations 'satisfice' (rather than seek to maximize profits as in classical theories of decision-making and micro-economics). Taking this view, routines are the outcome of negotiation between different interest groups within an organization. Routines thus represent a truce between interests and may be thought of as relatively stable rules and standard operating procedures for carrying out work and for 'refereeing' disputes between interests about how such activities should be conducted.

The notion of 'knowledge' should not be taken for granted within discussions of the nature and development of organization learning. As one commentator attempting to bridge the 'grey zone' between economics, organization theory and strategic management has noted: 'there is much [sic] silence on what ... precisely should be meant by knowledge and its management ... ' (Hedlund, 1994: 74). Whilst this is not the place for an all-embracing effort to solve this particular puzzle, some clarification of this often assumed and ill-defined notion is warranted. However, rather than offering a universal definition of knowledge, a more useful basis for proceeding will be to outline the common themes that tend to feature in contributions to the debate about knowledge, knowledge management and their relevance to organizational change.

The distinction and relationship between 'tacit' and 'articulated' (or 'explicit', or 'codified') knowledge is central to such discussions. This mirrors the distinction that has been developed around the difference between knowing, which is encultured, rooted in specific activities, expertise and contexts, and knowledge, which is symbolic and encoded. The classic definition of tacit knowledge is that contained in Polanyi (1962: 49), as cited by Nelson and Winter (1982: 77) and Winter (1987: 170–1) with respect to the nature of individual skills. Here, 'the aim of a skillful performance is achieved by the observance of a set of rules which are not known as such to the person following them'. As Winter (1987) notes the 'not known as such' and hence the tacitness of knowledge connotes the extent to which the person 'performing' is unable to explain in a usable way the rules of skilled performance to others, such that the recipient of the 'knowledge' would be as much in the know as the first performer.

Fully articulable knowledge, therefore, is that which is capable of such transfer and is typically described as codifiable or capable of being made explicit, as captured in a workbook or manual.

Arguably, the treatment of the relationship between tacit and articulated knowledge reveals a schism in the literature. Nelson and Winter's (1982) work exemplifies a preoccupation with the storage of knowledge. Their general concern is to explain through the notion of routines the automaticity of skilful behaviour and why organizations are slow to change. So, for Nelson and Winter the embeddedness of tacit knowledge and constraints on its articulation are primary foci. A somewhat different approach is to address ways in which tacit and articulated knowledge (or individual and organizational knowledge) interact, focusing upon the creation and transfer of knowledge. This view is represented by the oft-cited work of Nonaka on the 'knowledge-creating company', for example (Nonaka, 1991; Nonaka and Takeuchi, 1995).

For Nonaka, a critical distinction exists between 'Western', and especially American, stereotyped approaches to knowledge which emphasize codification and formality and those to be found in successful large Japanese corporations (though not exclusively). In the latter, the interplay between tacit and explicit knowledge is crucial to understanding knowledge creation. More specifically, the conversion of tacit to explicit knowledge may be characterized by four patterns of knowledge creation and transfer, which are enabled by various individual cognitive and organizational communication processes. These are summarized in Table 4.1 and are described in terms of the product development process at Matsushita. Here, one of their product development team (Ikuko Tanaka) was attempting to rectify problems with the design of a new bread-making machine by training with the head baker at a leading hotel in Osaka, near the firm's headquarters.

A number of salient issues pertain to the development of learning organizations through the enhancement of their repertoire of routines. The first of these concerns the overwhelmingly optimistic view of organizational learning that characterizes much writing on the topic (Borum, 1990). Coopey (1996) refers to 'learning Utopia' and Starkey (1996) captures the rhetoric of learning thus: 'The "learning organization" is a metaphor, with its roots in the vision of and the search for a strategy to promote individual self-development within a continuously self-transforming organization'.

Table 4.1 Four patterns of knowledge creation

Nonaka defines four patterns within the spiral of knowledge creation demonstrating the interaction of tacit and explicit knowledge:

1. Tacit–tacit: Tanaka learns from the baker's tacit skills through observation and imitation.
2. Tacit–explicit: Tanaka articulates this knowledge in a form that her colleagues at Matsushita can readily assimilate and share.
3. Explicit–explicit: the product developers at Matsushita are able to incorporate this knowledge into a workbook or manual which embodies the specifications of the new bread-making machine.
4. Explicit–tacit: the new explicit knowledge is internalized and shared by the employees, such that it becomes 'second nature' to them.

Souce: adapted from Nonaka (1991).

The benefits of such self-transformation typically are presented in terms of the capacity for maintaining the alignment of organizational activities with conditions in their external environment (fit again!). A view of knowledge as a strategic asset or 'competence' has gained currency. However, what Winter draws attention to is the need for some modesty concerning this position that knowledge and learning represent 'assets' or 'invisible assets' as Itami would put it. Two reasons for a less sanguine perspective are, first, that knowledge is not an asset in the balance sheet sense, since this conveys a notion of the possession of a discrete item or piece of property which is somewhat at odds with a view of knowledge based on individual tacit skills generated, and possibly shared, in specific organizational contexts. Second, the extent to which such individual tacit knowledge is not articulated or articulable casts doubt on whether this knowledge is transferable throughout an organization and hence whether it may be regarded as a strategic asset or competence (Winter, 1987).

The second issue is that the Utopian view of learning tends to underplay issues of control and politics. Such an approach emphasizes how constructive differences between organizational members are to the development of learning, where dialogue and mutual trust provide the means for resolution. A more explicit political approach might be taken with rather different conclusions about organizational learning.

In particular, there is a potential dilemma pertaining to the need to facilitate individual learning within organizations, on one hand, whilst on the other hand maintaining control over the efficiency of work done. So, an alternative view of the work of managers and leaders as regards the nurturing of the learning organization may be taken. Thus where Senge (1990) offers an optimistic portrait of the 'leader's new work', where this is to build what he calls 'generative learning' through envisioning future organizational missions and 'surfacing' then challenging the existing mental models of employees, a more familiar role for managers may be evoked. Here, managers are charged with the responsibility for developing the creativity, ingenuity and commitment of subordinates but also to regulate their performance against a backdrop of the need to control the costs of labour. And, against this, employees wield some countervailing influence through the regulation of their efforts and (potentially) what is referred to as their discursive capacity, which may be enhanced depending upon how 'informated' their work becomes (Coopey, 1996; cf. Zuboff, 1988).

A third set of issues concerns what structures or processes facilitate (or hinder) learning and knowledge creation processes. As Chapter 2 has demonstrated, there has been a great deal made about the benefits of certain structural forms and mechanisms for promoting organizational learning which will require reflection (see Chapter 7 on organizational restructuring). From a viewpoint that is claimed to be explicitly concerned with the management of organizational knowledge, a related prescription has been of the 'N-form corporation' (Hedlund, 1994), which bears more than a passing resemblance structurally to the kinds of new organizational structures suggested by Quinn (1992) in *Intelligent*

Table 4.2 Differences between the N-form and M-form of organization

N-form	M-form
Combines knowledge	Divides/specializes tasks
Temporary structures, long-term employment	Permanent structures, changing staff
Middle management critical	Top management critical
Top management facilitates	Top management monitors, allocates
Lateral communication emphasized	Vertical communication emphasized
Competes on 'depth' of knowledge	Diversifies portfolio
'Heterarchy' is basic structure	'Hierarchy' is basic structure

Source: adapted from Hedlund (1994).

Enterprise. (The central features of this N-form organization and the claimed differences between this and the 'Western' hierarchical 'M-form' are presented in brief in Table 4.2).

As far as issues of process are concerned, the socialization of new employees is seen as central to reinforcing organizational values and influential upon the internal exchanges that take place, including the generation and sharing of knowledge. Taking this view, Ouchi (1980) sees organizational philosophy as a mechanism both for asserting control over employees and for managing co-operation and knowledge-sharing. Particularly in uncertain environments, what Ouchi labels 'clan', rather than 'bureaucratic', management styles will be appropriate, it is claimed. Such clan management is associated with 'soft' contracting, in which mutuality of interest and trust between, in this case, parties to the labour contract is emphasized. Compared to hard contracting, where contracts are tightly drawn and there will be recourse to legal and economic sanctions between parties intent on pursuing their own sectional interests, soft contracting features more open contracts, since details of performance required may be ambiguous or unknown, and appeals to processes of social control (Starkey *et al.*, 1991). This kind of clan management and soft contracting has been identified with the employment and management practices of successful Japanese corporations in their Japanese operations. Since the late 1970s attention has turned to the transfer of such processes to the US and British plants of Japanese firms, and also to the managerial practices of US and British companies (Ouchi [1980] refers to the Theory Z organization which has absorbed some, if not all the features of typical Japanese organization).

Hedlund (1994) specifies a number of 'carriers' of knowledge to deal with another related issue concerning the degree to which there has been a preoccupation with internal organizational processes for stimulating learning, to the neglect of other wider sources of knowledge creation and development within industry sectors, networks or occupational communities. These operate at individual, work group, organizational and inter-organizational levels, though one is reminded that Burns and Stalker's

(1961) seminal work addressed the problems of knowledge creation in the Scottish electronics industry during the 1950s in a manner which embraced these levels of analysis and more, including relations with the State (Robinson and Clark, 1997).

A fourth concern addresses once more the 'down-side' of organizational learning. Organizational routines are regarded as the encoding of past experiences which serve to guide future actions. But their 'routineness' may suggest an embeddedness in the organizational fabric which might invite 'competency traps' where such routines become inappropriate to meeting external contingencies (Borum, 1990). In addition to this the notion of unlearning may be invoked to draw attention to a process whereby, as well as new knowledge being engendered and routinized, 'old' routines may (simultaneously) need to be supplanted.

Keeping in mind what has been presented on the subject of flexibility and learning, here, it is now possible to make connections to other treatments of change which further highlight the strategic significance of knowledge or routines and also generate an insight into potential sources of and barriers to their development. Examples of such other treatments include, first, institutional and, second, interpretive approaches to understanding change.

INSTITUTIONAL APPROACHES TO CHANGE

There are various approaches in economics and in organizational theory which adopt an institutional view of the management of change, where an institution may be understood as a convention that takes on a rule-like status in social thought and action (DiMaggio and Powell, 1991). Among these it is possible to define different branches of institutional economics, for example, which form the initial focus of attention of this section and to relate these to an explanation of why change might occur. For the purpose of this discussion the two aspects of institutional economics, concerned are: a) transactions costs economics, and b) evolutionary economics. Each of these is concerned with various kinds of 'institution' (which are said to govern behaviour in specific recurring situations in organizations). Transactions costs economics focuses upon contracts between organizations and how they relate to decisions about what activities a firm should perform in-house or buy in from others, whilst evolutionary economics emphasizes the significance of organizational 'routines', as discussed with reference to Nelson and Winter's work in the previous section. This section further considers Nelson and Winter's approach, which has as its basic orientation an interest in what makes firms distinctive from each other, alongside an institutional approach from within organizational theory, concerned with what makes firms similar or 'isomorphic' (DiMaggio and Powell, 1991).

Transactions costs economics

The theory of transactions costs which is advanced by Oliver Williamson (1975, 1979), for example, has the 'contract' as its focus. Contracts are considered by Williamson to be key to explaining the economics of alternative contractual modes (or 'governance structures') of organizations. How does this bear on issues of change? Well, the basic argument is that decision-makers in organizations will choose the structure which best economizes on transactions costs, having discovered (i.e. learned) the most efficient form of organizing . The application of this theory of transactions costs was originally aimed at explaining the growth of large, vertically integrated organizations through much of the twentieth century. Now Williamson's work has become an increasingly popular way of explaining the opposite – i.e. the restructuring of organizations and why deintegration or outsourcing may occur.

There are three contractual modes which are identified by Williamson, namely:

- the firm or 'hierarchy'
- 'mixed modes'
- the market.

Thus the basic choice for the firm is considered in terms of the 'make' or 'buy' decision, with 'make' relating to the firm performing particular activities, such as the design/manufacture of components or a finished product, in-house. The governing contract here is the internal labour contract which is set up so as to control efficiently the conduct of these activities. At the other end of the continuum stands the 'market', where arms-length, 'spot' transacting for the provision of various activities may occur. Here, there may be one-off contracts made with suppliers which have no special relationship with the purchasing organization. Between the 'firm' and the 'market' stand 'mixed modes' of governance (often referred to as 'intermediate' modes). These include franchising, outsourcing and subcontracting, and also joint ventures with rival competitors. In each of these variations on the mixed mode, the relationship, whether it be with suppliers or with competing firms is closer than in the pure market mode but stops short of the sort of hierarchical control that tends to associated with the pure internal mode.

Relevant to a discussion of change is why an organization might want to alter the mode of governance for a transaction. As mentioned above, it was with reference to the vertical integration of large corporations (in the US) that Williamson's transactions costs economics was initially applied. The example of the US railroad system in the nineteenth century is used by Williamson to illustrate a change in contractual framework from 'market' to 'hierarchy'. Once, the railroad system in the United States was characterized by a number of small firms (employing about fifty people) which operated railways of about fifty miles in length, sometimes in parallel with those of their rivals. In such cases of parallel lines being operated, one could say that this represented a market-based mode for running the system as a whole. However, it became increasingly apparent that parallel track would be superseded by longer lengths of track, laid end to end, with more people and goods travelling greater distances across the system. Contractual relationships between the owners of end-to-end track began to spring up so as to co-ordinate their operational activities and the bid to win customers for the system as a whole. This was a partial success, since the volume of traffic slumped during the 1870s as operators opportunistically engaged in price-cutting. The organizational response to this decline in fortunes was to be the merger of these operators and thus the integration of the system as a whole. Benefits to the system may be considered in terms of transactions costs savings on bounded rationality (since the merged operators could pool information on passenger requirements) and opportunism (through reduced price-cutting of the previously independent operators).

The transformation of Du Pont from a functional company structure towards a multidivisional structure has been cited as a case in point, this time to explain the change in structure of an already integrated firm. For Du Pont, problems of securing control over the goals and objectives of departmental managers grew as the organization as a whole became larger and more complex. In short, the functional structure of the firm became beset by the bounded rationality problem, since senior management was unable to absorb the vast amount of information flowing through the organization. Also, there was a problem of opportunism since functional departmental managers were increasingly pursuing their own goals, rather than ones which senior management had set for the organization. The benefit of a multidivisional form in this type of situation is said to be the potential for making economies on bounded rationality, in that strategic and operational decisions could be distinguished more neatly and allow for better definition of role between the central office and divisions of the organization. As well as this, greater transparency of resource allocation may be facilitated under the multidivisional form so that the corporate headquarters might better control the pursuit of subgoals by divisional managers which harm the efficiency or profitability of their division. Williamson considers Du Pont to be a diversified conglomerate, a variation on the multidivisional form, wherein the central office is contracted to act on behalf of the shareholder, and ensures that the performance of their investment is monitored and any changes necessary to improve cash flow from various operational parts of the organization are implemented.

Williamson's work on transactions costs emphasizes the economics of contracting and of the management of knowledge, embracing considerations of bounded rationality and opportunism, what he terms 'asset specificity' and the uncertainty and the recurrence of the transaction. The appeal to contractual imagery and the negative assumptions of human motivation implicit in its emphasis on opportunistic behaviour have been criticized (Kay, 1992). Features of a social exchange approach (rather than economic exchange) take us away from contracts, whether between a firm and its suppliers, or allies, or within the firm between the employer and

employees. Instead, there is greater attention to aspects of intra-organizational and interorganizational relations that are said to be implicated in
changing approaches to managing across organizational boundaries and
knowledge creation. To some extent it could be argued that these are
addressed by the notion of 'soft' contracting referred to earlier in this chapter, though this retains the contractual imagery complained of by Kay. He
is generally critical of the view that problems of contracting, and therefore
those giving rise to transactions costs, are economic and explained in
terms of market failure rather than being fundamentally social and political in character. A strategic network perspective, by contrast, emphasizes
behaviour over time among various producers, suppliers, governmental
and academic parties, and as such helps to move beyond the narrow con-
fines of the focal firm's approach to managing across its boundaries and to
explore the wider context of strategy and change. Arguably, the proponents of the network approach also adopt a more optimistic, processual
view of such relationships, highlighting the significance of trust and
mutual co-operation to interorganizational collaboration and learning.

The kinds of issues that tend to be of concern from a strategic network
view relate to both horizontal and vertical collaboration. Briefly, horizontal collaboration takes place between competitors (e.g. car manufacturers
at the same stage of the production process who would be regarded as
competitive rivals, and indeed still are even though they collaborate). Such
co-operation may be facilitated depending upon the role of non-corporate
bodies. In this regard, the role of *keiretsu* structures in Japanese industry in
promoting horizontal collaboration between firms is often held up as an
example of the benefits of close links between governmental, financial and
industrial institutions, conditioned by a complex of historical development and aspects of national culture. Vertical collaboration is a term
applied to relationships between suppliers and manufacturers and the sub-
contracting/contracting-out, or outsourcing of activities. The key point
here is the degree of mutual co-operation, the involvement and expertise
of the supplier, and the nature of the 'game' between the parties. A stereo-
typical representation of the latter is to juxtapose 'zero-sum' games
(emphasizing the parties' lack of congruent goals, opportunism and the
withholding of information) and 'win-win' games (emphasizing common
interests, trust and the generation and sharing of knowledge). Further, a
not uncommon contrast is made between 'Japanese' supplier relationships
(of the 'win-win' variety) and the traditional American/Western version
('zero-sum'), with a question mark added as to how the latter either should
change or has changed (e.g. Freeman, 1992; Jarillo, 1988).

Why are organizations different or similar? Evolutionary economics and institutional isomorphism

An alternative to the transactions cost approach, within the area of institutional economics, is suggested by Nelson and Winter (1982). For them the
institution that is of most significance is the firm as a 'repository of

knowledge'. Taking this view, explaining why organizational change occurs is a matter of understanding how the knowledge base of the firm relates to organizational 'routines'. As described above, these routines govern the ways in which repeated activities are performed and it is an accumulation of experience from various sources which permits learning of how to do those tasks better. Understanding change from this view points to the difficulties of changing routines which act as deep-seated rules of conduct at various levels in an organization

The main preoccupation of Nelson and Winter's evolutionary economics is captured in the title of an article by Winter in a collection of contributions published by Harvard Business School on fundamental issues in strategic management (Rumelt *et al.*, 1994). In the aforementioned volume Nelson addresses the question 'Why do firms differ?', the answer to which revolves around the distinctive capabilities and routines of different organizations (which search for potentially better ways of doing things). By contrast, the question posed by DiMaggio and Powell (1991) in their analysis of institutions aims to uncover 'why organizations are so alike?'

DiMaggio and Powell draw on the notion of institutional isomorphism, a term which is rarely invoked to illuminate organizational change within the strategy literature and, yet, which possesses an undervalued relevance to understanding contemporary organizational developments. Essentially, institutional isomorphism refers to the tendency of organizations within an organizational 'field' to adopt similar practices (these practices are the institutions in question). A field may be thought of as the totality of organizations and groups defining a community or 'societal sector' rather than an industry sector or interfirm network as conventionally understood. Further, institutional isomorphism may be distinguished from competitive isomorphism. The former term applies to the late adoption of new practices by 'follower' organizations, where some notion of it being legitimate for such practices to be employed plays a greater part in the process of change than reasoning based upon the pursuit of increased competitiveness. Competitive isomorphism, on the other hand, emphasizes the orientation of 'early adopters' towards the search for efficiency-enhancing improvements, new practices or processes which may improve their competitive standing (DiMaggio and Powell, 1991). Referring to the voluntarism–determinism (strategic choice) debate, the latter brand of competitive isomorphism recalls the more severe form of population ecology where, crudely speaking, organizations essentially have to adapt/imitate or die. The institutional version of isomorphism may be construed in terms of the modest strain of population ecology where organizations have some latitude to adopt new practices which appear legitimate within the cognitive arena that demarcates their field, even if such change does not have much to do with becoming more efficient, a point emphasized by DiMaggio and Powell. Recognizing this distinction between these two types of isomorphism raises a question mark against the motivation for some commonly made organizational innovations of recent times. Chapters in Part II of this book will consider this with reference to the extent to which the introduction into organizations of 'Japanese' production methods, or business process re-engineering, have been driven by efficiency and strategic considerations of competitiveness more generally, or by considerations of legitimacy. This deep-seated quality of what is seen as legitimate to do within organizations is captured by the notion of the organizational paradigm, a subject which will now be more directly discussed with reference to an interpretive approach to understanding change.

AN INTERPRETIVE VIEW OF COMMITMENT AND CHANGE

The following paragraphs seek to move beyond the various planned approaches to managing strategic change by putting centre stage an interpretive view of the process. What this means may be understood by considering organizational culture and change in terms of the values and beliefs which characterize organizations. Taking this view, understanding how and why organizations change (or, indeed, do not change) becomes a matter of capturing how various political, symbolic and structural factors condition the perceptions of individuals or groups of the current and potential position of the organization and its environment.

What Johnson (1987) refers to as an 'interpretative' view of strategy development and change emphasizes the centrality of the paradigm of an organization, a concept not distant from Weick's (1983) idea of a 'cognitive map' which describes the assumptions held by members of an organization and which condition their view of the organization's world. The paradigm consists of the core, taken for granted beliefs of that organization, which are commonly shared by its members, and which explain how it competes over time. The paradigm is integral to the cultural web of an organization and will be influenced by a host of factors (such as routines, myths' and symbols within the organization, the possession and use of power and organization structure). The task for the present is to bring out the relevance of an interpretive/interpretative approach to understanding strategic change. A good way of doing this is to reflect upon Johnson's work on organizational paradigms as applied to his study of Fosters, the British menswear retailing firm.

The research by Johnson focused on Fosters' strategy and market environment over the period 1971–86. In essence, the basis of competition of the firm over that period could be summed up by the phrase 'pile it high, sell it cheap'. There was an emphasis on the supply of workwear to down-market segments of the mens retail clothing sector. The strategy could be said to be underpinned by elements of Fosters' cultural web. Hence, fundamental to the paradigm of the firm during the time of the study was the perceived significance of bulk buying and the capacity of Fosters to retail cost-efficiently. Other critical aspects of the cultural web also related to the primacy of Fosters' merchandising function. For example, a key routine concerned the long-established practice of sourcing merchandising from the Far East, whilst the organization was characterized by the telling of stories about the big buying deals of its past. One more important ingredient in the Fosters culture pertained to the style and orientation of its senior management. The top-down nature of decision-making at Fosters is encapsulated by symbols such as the use of initials in referring to senior executives (and 'sir' to the chair of the board), by the rigidity of its control systems and a 'finger in every pie' approach. In addition, the inward-looking focus of the management is exemplified by stories of (extreme) staff loyalty to the firm and by the manner in which outsiders became marginalized or eased out of the company if they did not conform to accepted ways of seeing or doing things.

This last point is especially significant considering the changing market environment within which Fosters operated. The key development during the 1970s lay in the growing importance to Fosters' target market of fashionable merchandise sold in high-quality shop premises. In the first part of the 1980s, the overriding contextual economic factor was the severe recession of that time. It is illuminating to consider the relationship between Fosters' internal and external environments and how these bear on the management of strategic change within the organization. As Johnson is careful to stress, the story of Fosters is not so much about a firm that would not 'adapt' (his word). Rather, the point is to try to understand why changes that were undertaken by Fosters came to be adopted and implemented in the manner in which they were.

Clues here are generated by referring to how 'consonant' and 'dissonant' the interpretation of relevant environment signals is with an organization's paradigm. How such change is interpreted forms the basis of the organization's strategic actions. (Note that some changes in environmental conditions may be perceived as irrelevant. In the case of Fosters, the extensive refitting of Burton's shops during the 1970s was not considered relevant to their own operations, since Fosters' management felt that Burton were competing in quite a different industry segment).

Where changes in an organization's external environment are considered relevant and perceived as consonant with its paradigm, strategic action to deal with such change will be capable of being conducted within the organization's existing way of doing things. At Fosters, this is exemplified by the firm's response to the economic recession of the early 1980s. This comprised an emphasis on cost control, price competition and a greater sales force effort – comfortably within the bounds of the firm's paradigm. Even some apparently more radical strategic changes adopted by Fosters may be considered in terms of consonance rather than dissonance with its paradigm. Thus acquisition and diversification policy during the 1970s, into areas ranging from women's retail clothing to drugstores, reflected Fosters' confidence in their merchandising capabilities. These areas therefore represented to the firm targets for the application of the recipe that had worked so well within their traditional menswear market. In short, these were growth opportunities that were perceived as consonant with Fosters' paradigm.

The developing trend towards favouring higher-quality products and more aesthetically pleasing shopping environments, which had progressed during the 1970s, may be considered as dissonant with Fosters' paradigm. Attending to such developments would have necessitated actions at odds with the firm's dominant values. This indeed was recognized by Fosters' marketing director Richard Haynes. When, in 1981, Fosters' financial performance was in the doldrums, Haynes (a recent recruit from outside of the company) had formed a view of the firm's strategy based on market research that he had commissioned. The position Haynes took was critical of the dominant perception that Fosters' management held of their core market and how to compete in it. What is of particular interest at this stage is to note the challenge that Haynes presented to the established power base within Fosters, centred as this was on the merchandising function, and the form of their resistance to this perceived 'attack'. As Johnson observes with respect to other writings on this topic, it is to be expected that challenges to the dominant values of an organization will be met with counter-resistance and the reinforcement of that paradigm. At Fosters, the form of this counter-resistance may be considered as symbolic in that 'myths of retailing experience' were raised. Thus resistance to the perceived challenge of Haynes took the form of claims that as an outsider he did not understand the 'Fosters way' of doing things and that the market research had been commissioned by someone who clearly lacked the required degree of retailing experience. Arguments of this sort provided the rationale for simply ignoring the market research in question. The solidity of the Fosters paradigm helps to explain the firm's enduring commitment to existing ways of doing things and hence their reluctance to even contemplate strategic change beyond the bounds of the paradigm.

SUMMARY

This chapter has sought to outline some of the developments that have occurred in a range of academic disciplines which have produced some insight into the process of change based upon a concern for flexibility, learning and the management of knowledge. As the foregoing sections have shown, there needs to be recognition of a possible tension. This may be between the apparently altruistic concepts of flexibility and learning, the logical pursuit of which seems unquestionable, and practices for enhancing these capabilities which may represent vehicles for serving the interests of particular groups within organizations. In addition, the chapter has outlined a variety of 'institutional' approaches which may help to explain further aspects of change. The principal divide is between theories of economic exchange, such as transactions costs economics, which focus on the search by organizations for more efficient modes of regulating contracts, of which the internal labour contract is one, and theories of social exchange. The latter is represented by social and strategic networks approaches, which tend to emphasize the role of trust and knowledge sharing between and within organizations, rather than the costs of opportunism and bounded rationality that provides the target for transactions costs economics. Finally, it is as well to address the issue of why fundamental change tends to occur less than incremental change, or why imitative change may be favoured over iconoclastic change. To illustrate that part of the discussion much has been made of the embeddedness of organizational routines, and the idea of an organizational paradigm which may characterize the pervasiveness of ingrained practices and values which militate against change. The concept of institutional isomorphism was invoked to draw attention to how organizational innovations arise from other than competitive concerns and may have more to do with a range of external factors promoting imitation.

PART II
MANAGING CHANGE IN PRACTICE

AWARENESS OF ENVIRONMENTAL CHANGE $\boxed{5}$

INTRODUCTION

This first chapter of Part II of this book discusses various approaches to the conduct of environmental assessment and possible connections to the promotion of change in organizations. As with the remaining chapters of this part of the book, this chapter seeks to present theoretical explanations and empirical findings relevant to an aspect of change, within the context of the broad perspectives of managing change introduced in Part I (i.e. voluntarism, weak voluntarism/soft determinism and environmental determinism) More specifically, here, the questions that are being posed include the following: where does awareness of a need for change come from in organizations? What role does formal planning play in developing such awareness? Who is responsible for shaping views about the need for and nature of proposed change? What is the significance of such factors for competitiveness and performance?

The last of these questions directs attention to an important but sometimes neglected issue concerning assumptions about relationships between environmental analysis or awareness, the management of strategy and change, and some measure of the performance of individual organizations. Earlier chapters in Part I of this book have cautioned against simplistic one-dimensional accounts of such relationships, with particular regard to prescriptions for managing change in the pursuit of strategic or structural fit. An essential aspect of this chapter, therefore, is to shed light on how people in organizations construe or analyse environmental factors and their significance, based on a consideration of research on the topic, with recognition of the theoretical assumptions and limitations of these accounts.

Child's model explaining sources of structural variation (discussed in Chapter 2) provides a starting point for considering the work of the present chapter. The basic line of argument is that organizational change is driven by actions taken in the light of objectives and values selected on the basis of analyses or perceptions of the environmental conditions that the organization faces, and its ability to perform effectively within that context. Here, the following sections address analytical and processual explanations of the conception and development of environmental awareness. They consider the conventional wisdom that organizational change is dependent upon change in objectively analysed environmental conditions. There is an assumption of cause and effect here which needs to be challenged and questioned. Hence the concern in the next section with how decision-makers 'know' or think about environmental conditions, the problem of research on the incidence of formal analysis and forecasting of environmental trends, and the role of planning, planners and plans in organizational strategy and change. The critique made of the 'planning pays' literature by Henry Mintzberg is central. In the final section the focus shifts towards more subjective views of environmental awareness. Building on the previous section, the issues under consideration centre upon the moulding of collective 'sense-making' regarding the nature of external environmental factors and their relevance to internal organizational activities and performance. Drawing upon the work of previous chapters the interaction of external and internal organizational factors in shaping the character and realization of change is identified, with respect to an interpretive, politically sensitive, approach to organizational learning.

EVIDENCE OF FORMAL PLANNING

First, the role of formal planning and forecasting methods in the practice of environmental assessment is considered. It is not intended to describe individual planning techniques here owing to lack of space. (In any case, these are presented in most basic strategy texts). Rather, the point of interest is the difference between the exhortations of the proponents of planning that organizations follow their elaborate models of strategy formulation and the modest role that formalized, quantitative planning plays within developing environmental awareness in practice.

The brand of thinking being questioned here is that which fills the ample volumes of writers such as Ansoff and Steiner, the most ardent and persistent advocates of the planning approach to strategy formulation. The sophistication of this type of approach is exemplified by Figure 5.1. Taking this view strategic change is the product of a carefully controlled and deliberate process of analysis. The planner or planning department is assumed to play the central role in performing this analysis and is accorded central responsibility for the conduct of environmental analysis and the conception of strategy within the organization. Assistance with this work comes courtesy of a number of analytical techniques that have become closely identified with strategic planning. These include the well-known outputs of the Boston Consultancy Group, the PIMS database, General Electric and Royal Dutch Shell, between them have developed the product portfolio matrix, the experience curve, the directional policy matrix and scenario planning. These are but a few of the myriad tools of

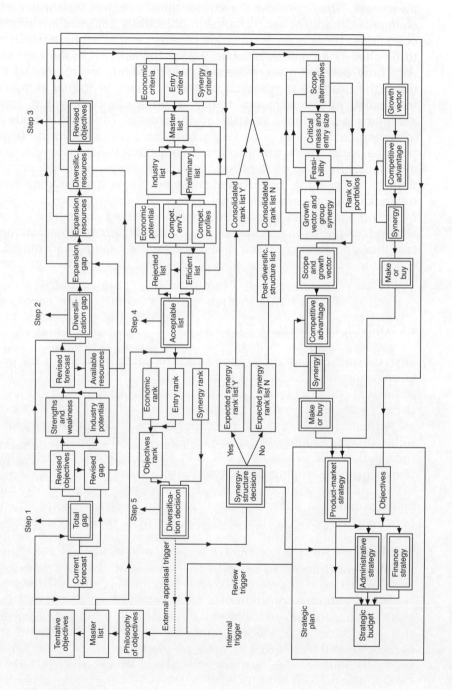

Figure 5.1 A comprehensive approach to strategic planning. *Source*: Ansoff (1965: 202–3).

the planner's trade and a number of statistics-based techniques for forecasting environmental or market conditions could also be quoted.

The first port of call for a critique of the work of proponents of planning is to question the validity of evidence of planning in practice. Summarizing Mintzberg (1994), certain distortions may be identified in survey research on the link between indicators of organizational performance and the conduct of strategic planning. These include:

1. **The unreliability of reporting**: low rates of response were being achieved with respect to mailed questionnaire surveys, with typically 20 per cent and sometimes lower proportions of samples of self-selecting respondents (i.e. the person with the title of 'Planning Officer' or similar) replying. Not only were such response rates considered unsatisfactory in themselves, the point at issue is the willingness of researchers to generalize freely on the basis of research so constructed, without apparently feeling a duty to acknowledge related limitations to the results of their work.

2. **The problem of measuring planning**: a conceptual difficulty signified by the absence or poverty of attempts to specify or define what was to constitute the 'planning' that was to be investigated.

3. **The problem of inferring causation from studies that were investigating correlation**: in other words, a tendency for researchers to mount studies to investigate the association of the conduct of planning with, say, the profitability of the organizations under scrutiny, but to end up with conclusions arguing that successful firms were successful because they relied on formally planned strategy. In any case, the idea that causation might also work the opposite way (i.e. 'rich' firms can afford extensive planning) tends not to receive the same attention in this literature.

4. **'Faith'**: where advocates of planning (e.g. Ansoff and McDonnell, 1990, ch. 3.2) cite only results which fit their view of the subject or acknowledge the existence of the contrary evidence but dismiss it, as in the following quotation from a consultant at A.D. Little: 'evidence like this does not say that planning has failed. Let's say that it just has not succeeded in ways that can be directly measured and credited to planning in the multi-variate corporate system' (Wright, in Mintzberg, 1994).

Taking all of this into account it is little wonder that Mintzberg (1994) comments on the 'soft underbelly' of hard data on the incidence of formal planning. What is of greater interest is the extent to which the less sophisticated techniques, and those which rely upon the subjective views of participants in planning, are employed in practice. Thus simple extrapolations of existing trends represent the most popular method of analysing or forecasting environmental trends, being employed in between two-thirds and three-quarters of US and non-US industrial firms and in US non-industrial firms (Table 5.1). Next in popularity comes brainstorming (used in 50–70 per cent of firms), followed by the use of statistical modelling (50 per cent approximately) and then a variety of qualitative and more quantitative techniques (Genus, 1995). In addition, there is another point to note concerning how techniques such as portfolio analysis, which are presented as offering some insight into corporate health based on 'objective' data on market growth and relative market share, depend in large part upon subjective definitions of an organization's market and its attractiveness (McKiernan, 1995). Further, it has been found that the accuracy of the more sophisticated techniques for forecasting is poor, feeding concerns about their validity for strategic planning purposes. The popularity of processes such as brainstorming and scenario-building indicates how organizations may be addressing internal views about the environment and future trends rather than relying upon mechanistic but flawed formal planning methods. More of this point will be made later in the current chapter. The following comments will suffice for now. First, formal techniques do not appear to drive strategy formulation and change as their proponents might wish. Instead inertia appears to be one of the characterizing pitfalls of strategic planning. Hence Mintzberg's observation of the inflexibility of planning (and plans) whereby the clear articulation of plans serves merely to breed resistance to change and the process of planning as a conservative, annual exercise leading to mechanical extrapolation and a lack of awareness of the need for even minor change. Second, the advocacy of 'flexible planning' as recommended by Gluck and Koontz for example (i.e. plan comprehensively but keep the planning process as creative as possible) is seen as a contradiction: 'it reduces the process to sheer confusion, or else, if recognised for what it is, simply folds into another process commonly known as management' (Mintzberg, 1994: 185).

If in practice the role of formal planning is not one of strategy formulation, what is it? One answer to this question comes, again, from Henry Mintzberg (1994), who considers that this role may be thought of as one of 'strategic programming'. Qualifying this point Mintzberg avers that in

Table 5.1 The popularity of different methods of forecasting

Method	Top 1000 US industrials (n = 215) %	Top 300 US non-industrials (n = 85) %	Top 500 foreign non-industrials (n = 105) %
Simple extrapolation	73	74	72
Brainstorming	65	69	52
Statistical modelling	48	51	45
Simulation	34	38	27
Trend impact analysis	34	31	29
Delphi technique	33	24	35
Cross-impact analysis	12	11	5

Source: adapted from H. Klein and R. Linneman (1984) 'Environmental Assessment: An International Study of Corporate Practices, *Journal of Business Strategy*, Summer, p. 72.

Note: Percentage figures indicate that respondents used the method concerned 'frequently' or 'occasionally'.

effective organizations the role of planning is connected to making strategy operational, to the articulation of 'intended' strategy so that this becomes 'realized'. Studies by Mintzberg himself on strategic programming at Air Canada and at Steinberg supermarket chain support the contention that planning is consequential upon strategic decisions as opposed to strategy being dependent upon the conduct of planning. At Air Canada strategic programming involved the detailed co-ordination of routes and flight schedules, amongst other operational matters. At Steinberg, planning at a firm that had been managed in 'entrepreneurial mode' for some time became necessary when it was decided to seek capital from external financial institutions. In this case, the plan that was produced was a document for external consumption and internally served merely to justify and to elaborate the prevailing strategic vision of the firm which was to expand into shopping centres.

Recognizing the poverty of evidence within the prescriptive planning literature on the conduct of planning in specific contexts, Mintzberg nevertheless describes a number of conditions necessary for, or facilitating, the conduct and effectiveness of strategic programming. These include industry maturity, where product and technological forms are stable; the control of capital intensive activities; large organizational size (and deep organizational pockets); and external control, by a parent organization requiring its subsidiaries to conduct planning reviews, an elaborated structure and tightly coupled (i.e. interdependent) operations.

To digress briefly, Mintzberg's specification of different roles for plans (the documents) as distinct from planning (the process) is at odds with the view of others on the subject and at times sits uncomfortably with his own. For example, he cites two functions of plans as being to communicate strategic intentions and specify operational tasks and to enable strategic control. The first of these refers to communication of strategy in more than just a public relations sense, for example to specify the tasks or responsibilities of internal employees or to inform external groups such as suppliers, which may be important to the realization of an organization's strategy. The control function may rely on informal rather than formal control systems (a point made elsewhere by Goold and Quinn, 1990). However, more than that, the role of a plan may lie in providing a basis for accounting for differences between intended and realized strategy (in recognition of strategy development as an emergent process). These functions do not seem all that different from the claims made by proponents of planning (the process), which Mintzberg himself quotes with reference to the views of various supporters of planning (such as Steiner, Ackoff and Ansoff), who claim in defence of planning that it is the process of planning that matters. Hence 'planning is not Utopia , only the road to it', and along that road, it is argued, a variety of positive spin-offs may be obtained, such as the development of intellectual skills, or the build-up of a valuable information database and so on. (Curiously enough, Mintzberg's view of the role of plans also seems to coincide with the advantages of formal planning (not plans) cited by those such as J.B. Quinn, who are otherwise critical of planning approaches.)

Similarly, one of four roles ascribed to planners, the planner as analyst, evokes a reference to Quinn's work on logical incrementalism, which is considered briefly below. Three other roles for planners are stated: as catalysts, where the role of planners is the advocacy of far-sightedness within the organization, though of learning processes rather than formal techniques *per se*; as the 'finders' of strategy, where their function lies in the interpretation of the pattern of strategy in the organization; and finally, but to a lesser extent, as 'strategists', where the role of planners may be undermined by their lack of involvement in organizational activities.

ORGANIZATIONAL LEARNING, PLANNING AND ENVIRONMENTAL SENSE-MAKING

The above view of the roles of planning in practice is well supported by the work of Quinn on logical incrementalism, and by Pettigrew and de Geus who each consider the contribution of planning and planners to organizational change or learning. What these writers share is a concern to understand planning activity as a process of enhancing environmental awareness by supporting the judgement and building the commitment of organizational employees.

In Quinn's (1980) study planners engaged in *ad hoc* studies and interventions in the process of developing strategy, making some use of formal planning techniques. Quinn sees formal planning as just one building block amongst a number of factors which contribute to fundamental change. For him, the formally planned view of strategy overemphasizes attention to quantitative factors and underplays qualitative factors linked to organizational power and politics which, in his words, 'so often determine strategy' and change (Quinn, 1991: 97). The role that formal planning plays in strategic development is considered on the basis of Quinn's study of ten multinational corporations, including Pilkington Brothers, Exxon and General Motors, which all had internal procedures for formal planning at the time of his study. Fundamentally, 'in a process sense', formal planning helps to stimulate broader based thinking ahead than would otherwise be the case in organizations and provides a pool of information which may support (but not determine) managerial decision-making. More directly, in 'a decision-making sense' formal planning techniques have a similar role to the strategic programming identified by Mintzberg in that their use helps to 'implement strategic changes once decided on' (Quinn, 1991). *Ad hoc* or special studies are employed by senior managers, Quinn argues, to foster creative thinking about environmental change and he quotes the establishment of devil's advocates into the planning system at various organizations and the commissioning of reports by acknowledged independent thinkers at Xerox in this regard (Quinn, 1982).

What Quinn sees as an important ingredient in logical incrementalism is viewed similarly by Pettigrew as a supportive secondary mechanism, facilitating the kind of approach to environmental assessment indicated above.

A key point, according to Pettigrew, is to recognize the difference between environmental assessment and awareness as a single-point activity, featuring annual planning exercises which are the domain of the professional planner and such environmental awareness as an organization-wide phenomenon. Empirical support for the latter conception of environmental assessment comes from longitudinal studies of organizations in a range of industry sectors, namely the automobile sector, book publishing, merchant banking and life assurance. In the automobile industry, for example, the cases of Peugeot Talbot and Jaguar are cited.

Prior to Peugeot's acquisition of Chrysler UK in 1978, the latter had suffered from a peculiar approach to developing views of environmental conditions. The personal commitment to expansion of Chrysler Corporation chief executive Lynn Townsend is cited as an influential factor in applying the growth objective of Chrysler UK's US parent to the British subsidiary. This is explained by the desire of Townsend for Chrysler to match expansion at Ford and General Motors but also, interestingly, with some recognition of industry-wide assumptions about continued growth in output. Nevertheless, the extent to which Chrysler UK subscribed to a high-volume strategy based upon this view is seen as extreme and as having near terminal financial consequences for the company.

The pervasiveness of the expansionist view of the environment and volume-led strategy was such that it persisted even after a failed attempt by government to rescue the company and the sale of Chrysler UK to Peugeot SA. A change of tack at Peugeot Talbot saw the emergence of a company with somewhat curtailed activities. For example, the workforce was reduced by 17,000 by 1982, the commercial vehicle operations were sold off (to Renault) and the Linwood and Dublin plants closed (in 1981). In addition, an expansionist view of the environment seemed unsustainable in the face of stagnant consumer demand and rising import penetration of the UK market, whilst the strength of sterling (which was a 'petrocurrency') was harmful to the value of export sales. As for the development of environmental awareness, 1980s saw a dismantling of the formal rules and manuals which had accompanied the Chrysler mass-market view. In its stead came a more informal process focused upon developing shared sense-making about the nature of the business and market environment through regular meetings of senior managers in executive committees, for example. Further, it is argued that the recognition of the need to bring the workforce 'onside' promoted a broader organization-wide approach to environmental awareness. This is exemplified by the decision to send every employee on a one-day course in 1987 to appraise them of the significance of the newly launched Peugeot 405 to the competitive standing of the organization in its market (Pettigrew and Whipp, 1991).

At Jaguar such a process of collective sense-making was also established following a period where the influence of a mass-market view was being felt. More specifically, during the 1970s, while Jaguar was part of British Leyland (BL) new corporate managers at BL were hired from Ford and sought to emulate the volume expansion of their former employers, even at Jaguar which was more accustomed to competing within a restricted luxury car niche. To make matters worse Jaguar was denied its own planning functions since these were transferred out of Jaguar and centralized at BL headquarters. The implications of this were:

> [an] assessment that was carried out at corporate level met stiff opposition from Jaguar. Little effort was made to reconcile the two views [of BL and Jaguar], to help Jaguar staff 'make sense' ... of [BL corporate management's] wholly different approach to the market.
>
> *(Pettigrew and Whipp, 1991: 122).*

The critical factor in Jaguar's survival and turnaround in the post-BL period in the 1980s is cited as being the company's newly found ability to understand its environment and to confront assumptions about the industry in which it operated. This included the conduct of a world customer survey by marketing staff which highlighted the new significance of product quality on the part of potential customers. In addition, a broader concept of the organization's boundaries was demonstrated by a greater willingness to keep up to date with contemporary developments by forging closer links with suppliers, dealers and users. For example, dealers from around the world were invited to the Brown's Lane plant to voice their opinions on product quality, and the firm's Manufacturing Technology Centre joined a number of user and supplier clubs. Finally, the 'black museum' represented an attempt to sensitize the workers on the factory floor to the strategic significance of poor product quality by dramatizing this in the form of a display of poor work which employees were encouraged to visit (Pettigrew and Whipp, 1991).

The connection between individual and collective sense-making and actions taken within organizations is therefore deemed to be central to managing transformational change and competitive performance. A similar message is conveyed by de Geus (1996) in his discussion of changing approaches to planning at the petroleum company Shell, though with less explicit attention to any performance benefits that this may have. Recognizing that within a period of thirteen years one-third of companies in the Fortune 500 industrials in 1970 had dropped out, and attributing this to their inability to 'learn and adapt', de Geus focuses upon how successful companies institutionalize learning and change, and what role corporate planning plays in this process.

Ultimately, however, de Geus's focal concern is with planning and learning at Shell but at no other companies, successful or otherwise. Nevertheless, he refers to the role of planners in challenging the mental models of operational managers and the translation by the latter of revised judgements about the basis of competition in the oil industry into everyday decision-making. Such challenging mental models have been outputs from scenario-building within the planning function at Shell, the content of which has included floating the spectre of low crude oil prices at a time when they were buoyant. Perhaps the most interesting feature of the discussion relates to de Geus's complaint about the slowness with which learning becomes institutionalized and incorporated into actions and the role of planners in accelerating the process. A large part of the problem seems to be linked to ineffective teaching, where planners attempt either to present new models with which their intended audience simply cannot identify, or are unable to do justice to months, possibly years, of work in condensed presentations to senior management.

According to de Geus, overcoming this difficulty at Shell necessitated a willingness to change or to suspend certain operational 'rules of the game', such as the timing and 'numbers' orientation of annual planning exercises. Moreover, the importance of playing games is emphasized. So, the process of sensitizing operational managers to the possibility of low oil prices involved their contemplation of case studies based on the scenario. Here, the managers were able to air their thoughts about what they would do and what the reaction of the competition might be under the new conditions. But de Geus is at pains to stress that this needs to be more than mere game-playing, the prospect of which is not likely to appeal to busy managers. To ensure that such games are built upon, an exploration of playing games through 'transitional objects' is being undertaken. In Shell's case this means using computer models as a means for storing the 'microworlds' that are the product of the mental models of individual managers and to 'play back and forth management's view of its market, the environment, or the competition' (de Geus, 1996: 97).

There is another view concerning such a portrayal of planning as learning. Although there will be more detailed discussion of this later in the book, for now it will suffice to note and to reiterate the critique that has been made of the 'learning organization' in the previous chapter. Thus, whereas de Geus (1996) and Senge (in de Wit and Meyer, 1994) either neglect issues of control and power or assume the 'leader's' role in developing learning organizations, others point to ways in which such thinking serves to underplay the politics of organizational learning. For example, one might distinguish between apolitical and political models of organizational learning (Coopey, 1996). In the former category is found the type of approach representative of the work of de Geus, Senge and others. Here the learning organization is unquestionably a 'good thing', and where there is tension or disagreement within organizations ongoing dialogue will see to the resolution of any differences. On the other hand, a more explicit treatment of the development of learning organizations as a political process might focus on the dilemma of control experienced by managers charged with eliciting employee commitment and encouraging creativity while controlling labour costs, for example, or identify the nature and sources of opposition to related developments (Coopey, 1996). This latter type of analysis is drawn upon in subsequent chapters of this book with regard to the assumptions underpinning and implementation of practices such as total quality management, business process re-engineering or empowerment.

Gerry Johnson's study of Coopers provides an interesting point of departure as regards the degree of empirical support for either formal planning or logical incrementalism while producing some insight into the difficulties of organizational learning (as previously considered in greater detail in Chapter 4). In short, there was no evidence found of systematic environmental analysis or scanning, clear objective-setting and evaluation of strategic options against objectives as prescribed by classical perspectives of strategy and change (Johnson, 1988). However, Johnson's account of strategic change at Coopers over the period 1970–83, while tallying with the work of Mintzberg and others on the limited role for planning in practice, takes issue with Quinn's findings of logical incrementalism.

Johnson warns against building too much on the espousals of senior managers who in interviews claim to be adopting a process akin to logical incrementalism, as might appear to be the case in the research on Coopers. Instead, closer inspection reveals the inability of logical incrementalism to explain patterns and processes of strategic change over time (Johnson, 1988). Rather, Johnson claims, strategic change is better seen (in context and over time) as promoted or inhibited according to the meanings attached to environmental stimuli and actions based on these. In particular, meaning is mediated through the paradigm of an organization. 'Deviant' interpretations of environmental signals are resisted if they challenge the core dominant beliefs held within the organization. Hence, a degree of homogeneity is produced regarding perceptions of external conditions and the range of plausible strategic actions and these, though incremental, may suffice in the absence of crisis. In this way, one may consider how environmental awareness or organizational learning might be impaired, even though decision-makers convince themselves that environmental sensing and organizational change are proceeding admirably.

SUMMARY

The sections above have taken issue with formal planning approaches to the link between developing awareness of environmental factors and organizational change and performance. As well as limitations peculiar to the 'planning pays' literature, there has been an abundance of accumulated research into the role that the experience and judgement of managers and others play in framing a sense of where organizations stand in relation to their 'environment'. Indeed, the extent to which people in organizations enact or create the environment around them, and the role of mental models and interpretive schemes in conditioning perceptions of what this is, take attention away from questions of what formal planning techniques are employed in practice and whether they work. Instead, greater scrutiny falls upon processes that condition collective sense-making and the pervasiveness of dominant interpretations of organizational well-being or malaise and environmental opportunity or threat. These are subjective conditions which influence awareness of the need for change and its potential options for change.

RE-ENGINEERING
BUSINESS PROCESSES
IN PRACTICE 6

INTRODUCTION

In this chapter, the potential benefits and difficulties of managing change through the implementation of novel operational processes and technology come to the fore. At issue is the strategic significance of advanced technology and the radical philosophies of total quality management (TQM), just-in-time inventory management and business process re-engineering. One could, if one were cynical, say that since the 1970s the foregoing have succeeded each other as the latest management 'fad' or panacea to leave the ivory tower and enter the workplace to little avail. Perhaps more soberly, a review of what factors help to explain different motivations and achievements in these areas may be undertaken. In doing so, it is not intended to deal with the subject of the management of advanced technology separately. Related issues pervade both the whole of this particular chapter and the next one, concerned as it will be to identify some informating (and not so informating) aspects of the deployment of technology amidst organizational restructuring. Instead, it is intended to say a few words now by way of highlighting some core ideas about managing technological change which may be applied in such a way as to guide thinking about the implementation of change centred around the processes mentioned above, as well as the forthcoming discussions of Chapter 7. Perhaps unsurprisingly, some of these remarks mirror comments made previously in this book about the management of change in general.

First, technology does not equal hardware. So, when reference is made to terms such as technological innovation or technological change, the point of issue will address the capabilities of physical artefacts but also the 'softer' aspects of these capabilities embedded in the social and organizational dimensions of 'technology'. Although it is tempting and all too easy to retreat to a view of technology emphasizing machinery or equipment, the significance of political or symbolic aspects of technology, as well as organizational arrangements should be seen as interdependent factors deserving equal billing in attempts to understand the adoption and implementation of new technology.

Table 6.1 Kondratiev long waves and sectors carrying generic innovations

Kondratiev wave no.	Period	Key sector(s)/innovation(s)
1	1793–1847	Cotton, iron
2	1848–1893	Railways, steel
3	1894–1939/45	Oil, chemicals, automobile, electrical
4	1940/6–1981(?)	Electronics, aerospace
5	1982(?)–future	Micro-electronics/telecommunications/IT

Source: compiled by author from Clark and Staunton (1993); Freeman and Perez (1994).

The second key point to make is that technological determinism should be avoided. Such determinism is implicated in the formulation and interpretation of some pervasive views of economic and technological development concerning the incidence of long waves at the macro-economic level (Kondratiev, 1976) and technology life cycles (Utterback and Abernathy, 1975) at the industry sector level. The extent to which contingency theories have posited a deterministic relationship between technology and organization has also been a source of contention.

The emergence of a post-Fordist paradigm is identified within long wave theory with the fifth Kondratiev wave. Kondratiev (1976) posited waves of economic activity spanning regular periods of about forty to fifty years, encompassing phases of economic growth, recession, depression and recovery associated with the business cycle. Briefly, the periods of these waves are summarized in Table 6.1, together with the sectors in which so-called generic innovations occurred (typically in the downswing of a previous wave) which sponsored the upswing of the subsequent wave. A key point of departure exists between different treatments of patterns of economic and technological development. On the one hand are approaches influenced by neoclassical economics which are concerned to track macro-level patterns of innovation, based on analyses of price movements for key inputs associated with the diffusion of generic innovations. As well as long wave models, this category of approaches includes various types of studies of the diffusion of innovation based upon analysis of the technology life cycle or the 'S' curve of innovation diffusion, for example. Between them these views exhibit a tendency to mount explanations of the process of innovation which focus on aggregate macro-economic statistics and assume a linear 'frictionless transformation'. Such approaches 'smooth the processes of innovation within the firm into stylised facts' and economists in particular have failed to address at all the internal organizational aspects of innovation and technological change (Clark and Staunton, 1993: 32).

By way of contrast one can point to a growing concern to uncover factors which ease or inhibit the diffusion an implementation of new technology at the organizational level and to capture more of the unevenness of the innovation process over time. Here, reference may be made to techno-economic paradigms, of which post-Fordism is (arguably still) the latest. The notion of a techno-economic paradigm refers to:

a combination of interrelated product and process, technical, organizational and managerial innovations [which entail] a radical transformation of the prevailing engineering and managerial common sense for the best productivity and most profitable practice, which is applicable in almost any industry.

(Freeman and Perez, 1994: 98)

As with the neoclassical view of long wave theory, the seeds of the new paradigm are sown in the downswing of the previous Kondratiev cycle. What is different is the degree of attention that is given to the 'structural crises of adjustment' at the macro-economic level as the new paradigm emerges and to the social and organizational factors connected to the varying take-up of aspects of the new paradigm within and between existing industry sectors (Freeman and Perez, 1994).

Contrary to neoclassical thinking, organizational decision-makers do not have perfect information about the costs and performance of the advanced manufacturing equipment, information technology and operational processes cited as components of the package of generic innovations associated with post-Fordism. This plus the prevalence of a range of other organizational and technical factors will ensure that the displacement of one techno-economic paradigm and the establishment of another in its place to be a gradual, uneasy affair, characterized by friction and trial and error. Acceptance of such a view qualifies the extent to which macro-level analyses of technological development and diffusion can be said to seamlessly translate into (or reflect) changes at the organizational level. Indeed, Abernathy revised his earlier work on the application of the technological life cycle to the automobile industry to account for the 'dematurity' of the life cycle in that sector, due to a range of innovations implemented in Japanese competitors. However, this recognition of organizational activity to reshape the life cycle (by introducing teamworking, TQM and just-in-time processes) is not to be confused with support for an unbounded voluntaristic approach to strategic choice.

In addition to the aforementioned issues of imperfect information, bounded rationality and transactions costs, a number of other considerations give a steer towards the middle ground of weak voluntarism/soft determinism. Puncturing the rational choice implicit in the voluntaristic perspective are considerations of perception, related to attitudes towards the risks and benefits of innovation (Loveridge, 1990). These have, in turn, been characterized by reference to discussions of the short-termism or far-sightedness of investment (in training, or the new equipment required to realize the innovation in question) and its evaluation, at the societal and organizational level (Hayes and Garvin, 1982). Further, there are institutional and contextual factors which need to be catered for. The Japanese 'success story' of innovation in the automobile sector owes much to external attributes and circumstances beyond the individual car firms, such as favourable exchange rates with the United States, or features of Japanese industrial policy and organization which have oiled co-operation within interfirm networks or foreign investment in export markets (the role of MITI, or *keiretsu* and *zaibatsu* structures, for example).

As discussed previously, routines may be viewed as institutions within organizations governing the performance of everyday activities, representing a kind of negotiated truce between various parties. Taking this on board, questions of the introduction and sustainability of innovations within focal organizations have a political, or control, dimension to them. The innovations discussed in the sections below all, in their various ways, have something to say about the politics, control and wider context of organizational change, connected to the issue of why and how to 'exnovate', or to unlearn existing practices. Much of what is said ought now to be conventional wisdom, drawing on the legacy of the socio-technical systems approach, or recent contributions on the 'integration barrier' to winning the much vaunted strategic benefits of advanced manufacturing technologies, for example.

These research streams open up issues connected to the zone of strategic choice that is available to decision-makers regarding adoption of new process technologies and those organizational factors which are central to successful implementation. For example, with respect to strategic choice it has been recognized that there is a range of possibilities concerning how to use and organize for advanced manufacturing technology such as flexible manufacturing systems (FMS). Hill, Harris and Martin (1997) point to the influences upon managerial choice within the diesel manufacturing and various capital equipment manufacturing firms included in their study. Most notable are perceptions about market requirements, in terms of the continued importance of price competition, and the significance of cost efficiency, such that questions about rates of return on investment and the control of product variety were to the fore in implementing FMS. (What is more, these concerns about trade-offs between profitability versus product diversity run counter to the conventional wisdom concerning the technology of the post-Fordist paradigm and applied both to firms that had already moved towards flexible production of small batches or were attempting to do so.) Bessant (1985; 1991) addresses the problem of fit between technology and organization, invoking the term 'simultaneous engineering'.

On the 'people side' key barriers to implementation of computer integrated technology are cited. As indicated above these involve aspects of the training and skills base of employees, 'counter implementation' (by middle managers, not necessarily the shop-floor workers), the aforementioned short-term approach to investment appraisal, and 'rigid' work practices and organizational structures. Such factors explain why incremental ('substitution') approaches to implementing new technologies are adopted in practice, resulting in 'islands of automation', rather than a more strategic (or 'integrative') perspective (Bessant, 1985; 1991). In contrast, there is a certain stubbornness about some prescriptions for change in the area of introducing what Storey (1994) calls 'new wave' manufacturing techniques and technology. This displays a reluctance to deal with insights on 'what is' rather than what 'ought to be'. Such considerations suggest a degree of caution regarding the applicability of prescriptions advocating radical innovations to displace existing routines, with limitations applying both to the experienced scope of change and to the durability of more thorough-going efforts where these are made. In turn, the following sections discuss the issues as they apply to the management of change through the implementation of total quality management, just-in-time methods of inventory management and business process re-engineering.

TOTAL QUALITY MANAGEMENT

It is difficult to uphold any one single authoritative definition of quality. However, if only to provide some means of going forward with this discussion, the following characterization is of help. Bessant (1991) describes quality in terms of a product's excellence, reliability and fitness of purpose. So, the technical excellence of a Rolls-Royce is not something many would dispute; the same applies to the acknowledged excellence of Marks and Spencer's service. Reliability is all but assumed from Japanese cars. And as for 'fitness of purpose', a clear expression of this aspect of quality lies in the consumer protection legislation which defines this as a condition of sale which, if not fulfilled, entitles the purchaser to a refund or a replacement.

In addition to the above criteria, one may refer to the design of a product and the extent to which its manufacture conforms to the specifications laid down in that design so that the overall level of quality associated with a product is the sum of the 'quality of design' plus the 'quality of conformance' with that design. The design of a product may be thought of as the setting of the technical specifications of the product linked to a view that the manufacturer has taken of what product attributes are demanded or needed by potential customers (i.e. external considerations). The issue of conformance on the other hand may be thought of as being more to do with the development of internal process capability and quality control which should enable the product's technical specifications (as laid down in its design) to be achieved consistently.

Making connections between the management of quality and competitiveness, the strategic significance of quality may be argued with reference to the potential of good quality management to increase differentiation, to reduce costs and to increase productivity (cf. Porter). Since differentiation as a concept is evidently connected to high or even unique levels of quality associated with the product of a particular organization, this section will focus more on the efficiency/productivity arguments for increased attention to quality management. Here there is a need to consider the costs of quality.

It may be tempting to equate the costs of quality with those costs incurred in setting up and maintaining a quality control department. However, Crosby (1979) considers these costs as the 'tip of the iceberg'. Indeed, the total cost of quality to an organization may comprise the following factors: disruption to production; time and resources spent in correcting mistakes; materials, energy, resources committed in producing the original mistake; investments in inspection and other specialist activities required to track down and account for quality problems; customer returns or warranties; and poor customer relations and costs of corrective promotions and advertising. In sum, overall quality costs may be said to consist of two types which are incurred in the prevention of and checking for mistakes, or incurred in the failure of the above procedures.

The notion of TQM emphasizes the benefits of adopting an organization-wide philosophy reflecting a concern to reduce the amount of costly inspection and correction of mistakes in product manufacture, by taking a 'prevention rather than cure' approach. The benefits of such a philosophy may be illustrated. What follows is a look at two examples of the implementation of total quality management approaches at Xerox and at Hewlett-Packard, which are presented in terms of direct cost savings in scrap levels, time and resource use, and additional longer-term advantages such as improved customer service and satisfaction and competitiveness.

At Xerox Corporation, the US firm known for its photocopier and reprographic products, the background to introducing total quality management was declining performance as measured by a fall in the firm's market from 18.5 per cent to 10 per cent between 1979 and 1984. By 1988 this had recovered to nearly 14 per cent, an improvement due largely to efforts in the TQM arena. In particular, an important element of the process of change has been identified as Xerox's benchmarking with its Japanese subsidiary Fuji-Xerox. Initially, a number of criteria were established and reflected aims of the first stage of the programme, such as the number and quality of suppliers, indicators of product performance and so on. In addition, emphasis was placed on encouraging all staff to see themselves as responsible for quality and authority to stop the production line was devolved to non-management employees. The benefits from the programme included an improvement in overall product quality by 93 per cent (as measured by defects per 100 machines made) and the reduction of manufacturing costs by 50 per cent through better product design. Customer satisfaction was reported as being significantly increased. Moreover, the number of suppliers was reduced from over 5,000 (1982) to about 400 (1989), and reject rates for incoming components were reduced to a fraction of their figure. In one sense the most significant comment about all of this is that it was felt that a process had now been established which would support further continuous improvement in quality (Bessant, 1991). So far, so good.

Turning to Hewlett-Packard, a similar story is apparent but with quite an interesting twist as far as an appreciation of longer-term problems of change is concerned. The principal player featured is the Japanese joint venture operation, Yokogawa Hewlett-Packard. Here, performance had been poorer than other Japanese competitors in the late 1970s, as well as that compared to other Hewlett-Packard plants world-wide. However, by 1982 Yokogawa had won the Deming prize for quality having focused upon the quality of its product design and engineering. The twist in the tale occurs in the late 1980s when the pattern of improvement began to level off. What had not been recognized was the extent to which there was still an inward- rather than outward-looking focus and the need for a shift from internal to customer-oriented perceptions of quality (in terms of fitness of purpose) became the new preoccupation for the firm. The pressing issue now was seen as the management of a fundamental change in corporate culture for a company that had been founded on its technical excellence.

Moving on to the subject of quality circles, one can point to an area of much more limited change than suggested by the total quality manage- ment movement. In concept the quality of circles addresses the building of *esprit de corps* amongst groups of employees and this may enhance learning and problem-solving within the production process. In the UK, at least, the evidence is of great difficulty being experienced in their imple- mentation. For example, a study by Storey (1992) tells of the troubled industrial relations history of companies in the automobile sector and what this has meant for the fate of quality circles. At Rover it took eigh- teen months to set up twenty quality circles yet none were implemented in the key and contentious area of vehicle assembly. In one exemplar orga- nization (Eaton Ltd) the need for an amenable atmosphere regarding industrial relations saw the suspension of quality circles during the annual wage negotiations. In addition, the impact of managerial resistance on the implementation of quality circles is noted. At Plessey Naval Systems, for instance, middle managers 'killed off' quality circles which seemed to threaten and to usurp their role (Storey, 1992).

JUST-IN-TIME INVENTORY MANAGEMENT

Again, this section discusses strategic change through the eyes of one of the key techniques or programmes for change associated with the Japanese business successes of recent decades – just-in-time (JIT) inventory manage- ment. Three aspects of JIT implementation will be contemplated, centring on the diffusion of JIT in practice, experience with the introduction of JIT and the identification of potential obstacles to the successful implementa- tion of JIT.

On the matter of diffusion, the extent to which JIT is being taken up (at least in Britain), one may refer to Oliver and Wilkinson's 1987 and 1991 studies (Oliver and Wilkinson, 1992). Their sample of manufacturing com- panies revealed a take-up rate of 64 per cent in the earlier study while the 1991 research showed that the figure had grown to 82 per cent. Voss and Robinson (1987) had earlier produced a qualification to the diffusion rate quoted by Oliver and Wilkinson's 1987 study by declaring that only 20 per cent of firms which had said they were going to embark upon implemen- tation of JIT had major programmes underway. Thus, from this point of view the story (at least then) was one of piecemeal incremental implemen- tation. Similarly, qualifications may also be made to figures reporting the successful implementation of JIT. One reading of the Oliver and Wilkinson work suggests that as many as 90 per cent of firms implementing JIT were enjoying 'success'. However, closer inspection reveals that experience in the area of reducing set-up times, which is after all essential to the JIT idea, is less rosy. Although two-thirds of sample companies were seeking gains in this aspect of JIT, only 'moderate' gains were being reported.

Oliver and Wilkinson (1992) offer two examples to tell quite different stories of experiences with seeking savings in set-up times. The case of Cummins Engine Company represents the 'up side'. Here, the firm had established 'Set Up Reduction Action Teams', which comprised small groups of employees who were given training in the principles and concepts of just-in-time and of its role in the wider context of remaining competitive. The idea behind the teams was that they would discuss ways of potentially saving time to set up machinery on the shop floor and take the necessary action to implement new setups. The process was accompanied by open videoing of the discussion meetings and different machine setups, with care being taken to make the videoing and the videos the 'property of the team'. Ideas were reported as flowing 'like water' and the savings in set-up time deriving from this process was of the order of 75 per cent, achieved within a period of a few weeks from the start of the programme.

Another, more pessimistic, experience is that of a company known simply as 'an Engineering Company'. In this firm the implementation of JIT, through reduction of setup times, was an altogether more difficult episode, one characterized by great resistance to change. The basic problem, in this example, appeared to stem from two linked factors: a) the feeling on the part of machine setters that they were having time and motion study 'done' on them; and b) the perception on the part of the shop floor that their 'space' was being invaded – in other words setups were their responsibility and they did not appreciate management stepping on to their traditional territory. The extent to which the machine setters at this company were unwilling to commit themselves to what came to be seen as management's encroachment on activities that were traditionally the preserve of the labour force was compounded by the withdrawal of trade unions from the joint groups which were supposed to be overseeing change in this area.

Turning now to the implementation issues associated with JIT, the subject of performance measurement provides one key aspect of the management and evaluation of JIT programmes for implementing change. Crucially, the orientation of traditional accounting and finance functions in Britain may be criticized. A basic problem that has been cited again and again concerns the preoccupation of these functions with providing data to be interpreted by City institutions and stock market analysts, often having a short-term view of the firm's operations and investment, it is claimed, rather than with providing information in a way that better reflects long-term organizational health or customer needs. On this argument, potential improvements accorded to the firm by the implementation of JIT actually end up being penalized instead of being rewarded. An example of this is where reductions in the size of batches of production, one of the claimed benefits of JIT, are conventionally reported as requiring longer setup times and thus appear to reduce efficiency instead of improving overall effectiveness. Moreover, the true costs and wastefulness of existing modes of production are not fully captured by traditional methods of measuring productivity (Bessant, 1991).

A second issue that has already been referred to in this section concerns employee relations. Here, conflict with employees and trade unions on the matter of changes to their existing practices and roles stands out, as the marked contrast in the experience of Cummins Engineering Co. and 'an Engineering Company' reveals . So, too, does the issue of changing the basis of remuneration. The move to group/team-based rewards where formerly payment was on the basis of individual effort can be a difficult one. Some of the factors that require attention in this regard relate to the development of trust within particular teams or workgroups, the design of reward systems that are transparent and easy to communicate and, at the risk of repetition, the involvement and co-operation of those to be affected by the new system in its design (Bessant, 1991).

One dimension of the implementation of JIT that has not featured in this discussion so far is the relationship between firms, particularly with respect to supplier relationships. Just-in-time 2 (JIT 2), as the interfirm version of JIT inventory management is known, relates to the management of the supply chain and of the quality and timing of inputs into the producing firm's (or retailer's) value chain. In theory, the development of JIT 2 rests, in part, upon the definition of a few key suppliers by the producer. These central suppliers ideally will be certificated for the high quality of their outputs and the relationship between producers and suppliers will be one of 'mutuality'. Here, the move is away from traditional zero-sum, low trust Western supplier relationships towards Japanese 'win-win', high trust collaboration between suppliers and the firms to which they supply. A major survey by Ingersoll has shown that the practice of interfirm relationships related to the question of a transition to JIT 2 was some way short of the ideal. Hence 'key' suppliers were not being identified (respondents to the survey averaging over 300 suppliers each) and barely half of company suppliers were accredited for high quality achievements. What is more, the quality of the interfirm relationships was such that less than 10 per cent of respondents in the survey could declare that a mutual approach towards managing the supply chain obtained. All of this contrasts quite starkly with the supposed requirements of JIT 2.

BUSINESS PROCESS RE-ENGINEERING: MYTH OR UTOPIA?

One of the 'hot' management topics of recent years has concerned business process re-engineering (BPR). Essentially, two perspectives of re-engineering may be defined, each with implications for the management of change. These are a) a rational view of business process re-engineering which demands radical change, and b) business process re-engineering as a political process emphasizing more gradual change.

The rational perspective underpins the writing of gurus on BPR such as Hammer and Champy (1993). According to this type of view the implementation of re-engineering is imperative; without it firms will lose the competitive game. Even to keep up with the Joneses quite painful, radical surgery needs to be performed on an organization, it is argued. Such transformation applies to the norms and traditions of an organization and also to the managerial styles employed within it. As Willcocks and Grint (1997) put it, this view of BPR is about 'deracination'. In other words, re-engineering efforts are not merely the rejigging of existing activities and practices but require a complete rethink of business processes and operations. More specifically, the process of re-engineering touted by its proponents involves redesigning the firm's activities so that they reflect an orientation towards the customer's needs rather than those of the producer, or of particular functions within the producing organization. Moreover, BPR is viewed as an organization-wide and hence an essentially strategic activity. The holistic nature of the concept of BPR is thus captured in the extent to which a cross-functional and radical reorientation of the firm is required.

The rational view of BPR says little about the political nature of organizations except in the sense that the benefits of BPR are so transparent that there should be little conflict within the firm concerning what is required. The firm must adapt or die and the objectives of those who work for an organization, or who are its stakeholders, are assumed to concur. In other words, a unitary view of the mission, purpose and needs of the firm is entailed in this perspective of re-engineering. This is an area where the rational view of BPR attracts criticism, bearing in mind what previous work has shown about the politics of organizational life and of the practical difficulties of realizing radical strategic change.

However, the second perspective of business process re-engineering addresses a more political version of the notion. In seeing BPR as a political process, activities which underline the negotiation of change and the management of commitment in support of change come to the fore. Studies by a number of researchers have found that these issues of commitment apply to different stages of the introduction of BPR. Thus on one hand, there have been problems of achieving a consensus among employees and managers over what form BPR introduction should take. As well as this, on the other hand, practical difficulties have been experienced in making the move from the planning of BPR to its implementation, where the latter requires continued commitment to the changes that might be involved. In particular Willcocks and Grint's survey of BPR implementation shows that two of the three most cited barriers to success in implementing BPR are a) middle/line management resistance, and b) lack of commitment or less than enthusiastic support from top management. One other contentious issue concerns the symbolic role of information technology in facilitating or hindering BPR. A positive view of information technology (IT) in BPR implementation would be to see it as the engine of progress and change. However, a rather more negative picture of the politics of change is given where the visibility of equipment leaves IT liable to be the butt of criticism and even cynicism regarding the benefits of BPR, and hence one source of resistance to implementation.

Ultimately, however, the 'Achilles' heel' of BPR has been its proponents' treatment of the human beings at the centre of the process 'revolution', in spite of belated attention from Hammer (1996) to the 're-engineering of management' and work within 'process-centred' organizations. Aside from the language of re-engineering, suggestive of a technical fix for organizational ills which does not sit well with the valuing of human resources, there is the little matter of making sense of and applying the universal BPR message within organizations operating in peculiar circumstances (Willmott, 1995). In their haste to jump on the BPR bandwagon, executives abandoned a tried and trusted approach to organizational redesign, the socio-technical school, in favour of a new fad which ignored 'soft' issues such as the quality of working life and prevailing values and relations (Mumford and Hendricks, 1996). And this is part of the story of change since human beings do have an ability to circumvent, undermine or oppose what they consider to be illegitimate or unworkable. It could be said that a rather different part of the story is that the successes of re-engineering are counted in terms of how better integrated tasks (or processes) become and the greater empowerment of employees. However, these should not be confused.This improvement in integration and co-ordination of work may be desirable but it is not the same as broadening the scope of autonomy or the variety of work that employees enjoy (Willmott, 1995).

Implementation also flounders where 'the daunting task' of re-engineering is handed on by corporations to outside consultants. Of particular note is the lack of a specific detailed methodology for 'how to do re-engineering' in the words of its proponents, who favour instead rather generalized accounts of organizations that have been successful with 'it'. This has left room for consultants to repackage their existing techniques and solutions as re-engineering. Moreover the boom in demand for their services meant that often newly hired MBAs with little experience of managing major change programmes were being sent into client's offices or factories, exacerbating the potential for ill-attention to the expectations and circumstances to be confronted (Mumford and Hendricks, 1996). To make matters worse the claim has been made that in US industry, at least, managers could hide behind the rhetoric of re-engineering and in so doing avoid taking the blame for what were in effect cost reduction exercises by way of large-scale redundancies. Thus, despite Hammer and Champy's protestations that BPR should not be seen as another term for restructuring, the recipients heard the message they wanted to hear (Mumford and Hendricks, 1996). Moreover, change that has been perpetrated in the name of BPR has an isomorphic ring about it. The tendency towards imitation of the actions of others has been noted in connection with the rise of BPR and so too has the failure of many such change programmes (though one should exercise some care regarding the imprecise labelling of various re-engineering/restructuring efforts). As with some of the companies featured as exemplars in *In Search of Excellence* (Peters and Waterman, 1982), some of Hammer and Champy's star organizations claimed to epitomize the fruitfulness of the re-engineering approach, such as Hallmark cards and Mutual Benefit Life, have since performed less than glowingly.

SUMMARY

The variety of innovative operational processes and advanced equipment discussed here have tended to be associated with prescriptions for radical change, to enable the early and sizeable accrual of their claimed benefits. They have been in the vanguard of techniques and innovations that appear to signify the emergence of the post-Fordist paradigm, measures which could attend both to efficiency and to quality of product and service if implemented successfully. But the research shows where there have been problems. Even undoubted successes in quality improvement are not necessarily sustainable and experience in other areas reflects the degree to which implementation is incremental and falls short of the uprooting of existing practices advocated by proponents. The idea that somewhere along the line issues of employee management or historical industrial relations should feature as explanations for this is not exactly surprising. Perhaps what is surprising is that certain ideas, such as business process re-engineering, should have become so much flavour of the month without due attention to social and organizational factors.

ORGANIZATIONAL RESTRUCTURING AND THE MANAGEMENT OF HUMAN RESOURCES 7

INTRODUCTION

Thus far chapters in Part II of this book have addressed sources of awareness of the 'need' for change, and connections between operational activities, strategic performance and change, while embracing aspects of the voluntarism–determinism debate. Moreover, these chapters contrasted the rhetoric of radical and planned change, as associated with the advocacy of Japanese management processes and business process re-engineering, with the more modest tactical or incremental nature of change in practice. In this present chapter, an appreciation of these themes is applied to the topic of organizational restructuring.

Revisiting previous discussions in Part I brings into focus the nature of, and transition to, so-called flexible or post-Fordist organizational structures and processes. Salient and topical dimensions of the discussion here are the extent of a strategic perspective underlying major restructuring efforts, and the implications for knowledge management of such moves. Also implicated are questions about employee autonomy and creativity, linked to a concern about the development of human resource management (HRM) approaches to employee relations wherein employees' knowledge, commitment and flexibility are regarded as key to organizational performance. In general, to take Hyman's (1991) point, it is necessary to balance talk of flexible organization with some exposition of what labour market and other 'rigidities' are maintained. Further, one needs to set this analysis within the context of prevailing and changing power relations between management and employees, recognizing the differential influence over matters of strategic choice and direction that may apply to these groups. In Hyman's terms there needs to be a consideration of who gains and who loses from any restructuring at the organizational level, related to a critique of claims about the emergence of empowerment or flexible employment practices.

A similar concern might be voiced with regard to developments at the interfirm level. Here, the issues at stake include the extent to which the downsizing or vertical disintegration of large corporations concentrating on core activities has translated into 'shamrocks', 'flexible specialization', or 'dynamic networks'. Relatedly, such a consideration begs questions bearing upon the contrast between the opportunism of Williamson's portrayal of interfirm modes of governance and the emphasis on trust and mutuality featured in contributions to the literature on the development of strategic networks. In this area, but also where organization-specific matters are involved, the work of Quinn on intelligent enterprises provides a starting point for discussion.

The following section describes various flexible forms of organization defined by Quinn as responses to changing competitive requirements. These emerge, he says, with the need to better manage the knowledge pertinent to improving delivery of the intangible service element of the offerings of both service- and manufacturing-sector organizations. Thus he analyses the development of 'infinitely flat', 'inverted' and 'spider's web' organizations, of which more presently. Subsequent sections then offer alternative thinking on the issues raised. So, for example, the enhancement of management control, rather than the increasing empowerment of employees is among the topics addressed in the third section, as is the 'upsizing' (as opposed to downsizing) of organizations, partly due to fears of the loss of organizational memory. And, in the final section, the end of the chapter offers quite a different view of core-periphery labour, outsourcing and interfirm relations issues from that which Quinn (1992) offers. As will become evident, while the attractiveness of notions of flexible and learning organizations is acknowledged, a degree of healthy scepticism regarding the emergence and achievements of flexible forms of organization pervades the chapter.

ORGANIZATIONAL RESTRUCTURING

The primary issue here concerns those aspects of strategic change that are best characterized by reference to their structural form. Some of the factors which are commonly cited as driving changes in the structure of organizations have already been identified both in the introduction to this chapter and in greater depth in Chapter 4. In attempting to achieve better 'fit' and sensitivity to external demands, it has been argued, many large organizations have undertaken major restructuring in recent years. The new organizational forms that have arisen from this process have been described as promoting a) 'infinitely flat' organizations, b) 'inverted' organizations, and c) 'spider's webs'.

The development of the infinitely flat organization may be associated with the practice of delayering – in other words the removal of what are regarded as superfluous levels of hierarchy from within an organization. In the view of Quinn (declared in *The Intelligent Enterprise*), the role of technology may be to 'informate' work so that knowledge is dispersed

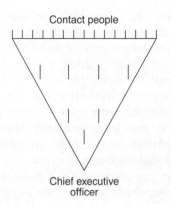

Contact people

Chief executive
officer

Figure 7.1 The inverted organization. *Source*: adapted from Quinn (1992).

throughout the organization and is available where it is needed most, in serving the customer. This is seen as critical to the development of the truly 'flat' organization, since the benefit of advanced communication and computing technology would allow increased spans of communication, with disparate parts of the organization being able to access data and each other through networked information systems. Thus the process of change that occurs is one in which there are fewer tiers of management, the number of managers relative to non-managerial employees is greatly reduced and, above all, the relationship between managers and subordinates develops such that the management of information and knowledge is of higher priority than 'old-style' close supervision and control.

The related notion of the inverted organization embodies and indeed emphasizes the significance of a customer orientation for organizations. Here, the conventional way of viewing the organizational chart is rethought and redrawn. The key issue concerns the roles of line and staff functions. Figure 7.1 demonstrates the importance of empowering those who have closest and most regular direct contact with the customers of an organization. It is these people, who may occupy sales positions or apparently modest roles in delivering everyday service to customers, who need to be well supported in their front-line efforts by the rest of the organization, including the chief executive officer. Of course, achieving this kind of reversal of roles would suggest quite a dramatic rethink of organizations and their processes.

An illustration of such intelligent enterprise is provided by the example of Federal Express in the organization of their parcel courier delivery business. Quinn cites a number of factors which he says have contributed to Federal Express's capacity to achieve cost-efficient operations, while maintaining the reliability and innovativeness of its service to customers. Central to these capabilities are the firm's information management technology, aspects of its organizational structure and design, and the strength of its core cultural values. Quinn describes the 'COSMOS' (Customer,

Operations, Management and Services) and 'DADS' (Digitally Assisted Dispatch System) systems into which are fed details of the sender, the item(s) being sent, the address of sender and recipient and the specific service required. These systems also help to co-ordinate Federal Express' delivery activities through the monitoring and scheduling of the organization's aircraft and delivery van fleets (the latter vehicles having radio-controlled units linking couriers to dispatching centres, for instance).

As well as employing the equipment just described, Federal Express's 'unique' organizational practices are fundamental to its capabilities. The flatness of its organizational structure is evidenced by there being five layers of hierarchy between the employees at the 'bottom' and the chief executive at the 'top' (cf. Peters's advice cited in Chapter 3, p. 36). Quinn also emphasizes the spans of communication (rather than of control) within the company. Whereas the legacy of Taylorism dictated spans of control of one manager or supervisor for every eight or nine subordinates, the automation of information distribution allows 'intelligent' organizations, like Federal Express, to operate with spans of communication of one manager to twenty front-line employees, or more.

The last piece in the jigsaw concerns the Federal Express motto: 'people-service-profit'. This is quoted as encapsulating the firm's customer orientation, as referred to above with regard to inverted organizations. The practical expression of this mission statement lays in the encouragement of employee participation throughout the organization. This is exemplified by self-managed work teams which are said to perform many functions formerly associated with management, such as performance appraisal and work scheduling, and regular 'bag' lunches attended by employees and senior executives which generate suggestions for improving quality and productivity (Quinn, 1992).

(A certain amount of care is warranted here. Quinn provides a number of vignettes describing aspects of 'intelligent enterprise', of which Federal Express is but one. However, these are not detailed, methodical analyses of the case study organizations' practices. Nor are they historically- or context-sensitive studies that enable the reader to trace what processes of change have been undergone to produce the practices described, or to understand more fully why they have been undergone.)

The spider's web is similar to the infinitely flat organization but with one main difference. Where the infinitely flat organization is typified by interaction between subordinates and the local manager or centralized information system, rather than by horizontal relationships, the spider's web reflects the critical nature of horizontal interaction between units (or 'nodes') of the organization (see Figure 7.2). Further, the location of expertise and knowledge creation differs. In the spider's web, expertise and knowledge are generated from the operational units and the role of the centre is to co-ordinate and diffuse that knowledge throughout the organization, whereas in the infinitely flat organization expertise residing at the centre is the critical factor.

Quinn differentiates between two types of spider's web: 'skunkworks' and 'shamrocks'. Essentially, the skunkworks type of spider's web may be related to the pursuit of flexibility through the design of internal organizational structures such as the matrix or 'N-form', which may allow *ad hoc* teams to form and reform in order to resolve particular problems of innovation, for example. Such an approach reflects a cross-functional interaction amongst parts of an organization and the locus of authority resides with those who have greatest knowledge to bring to solving a particular (customer-oriented) problem. The same person may lead a team for one specific task yet become a subordinate within another team for another task.

One of the organizations said by Quinn to exemplify the cross-functional design of the skunkworks variant of the spider's web is Arthur Andersen & Co. As well as employee selection and training and the firm's information system (the 'AANET' system which links the office unit 'nodes' worldwide), the reward system is cited as critical to information sharing. At Arthur Andersen the role of local profit centres is de-emphasized; partners in the firm share in its total profits instead. Performance appraisal of employees seeking to become partners proceeds partly on the basis of the number of cases they submit for collective problem-solving. In addition, the evaluation of employee performance takes into account the frequency with which individual staff are sought to participate in a problem-solving team and how well they co-operate within such teams (Quinn, 1992). In general, the thinking underlying this conception of skunkworks draws upon Quinn's logical incremental approach. This is especially so in respect of the stress that is laid upon the inability of individual specialists, or dedicated functions, to solve complex problems. Instead, co-operation is highly valued and occurs within informal *ad hoc*

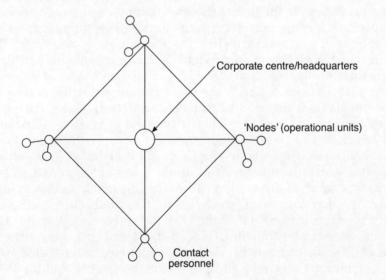

Corporate centre/headquarters

'Nodes' (operational units)

Contact personnel

Figure 7.2 The spider's web organization. *Source*: adapted from Quinn (1992).

temporary structures where authority follows those who possess greatest information, rather than mirroring the formal hierarchical structure of the organization.

The shamrock form is closer to the interorganizational network discussed with regards to flexible relations between firms in Chapter 4. Here, the three leaves of the shamrock represent the small 'core' workforce of the organization, its temporary or part-time 'periphery' workforce which grants a buffer for coping with changes in demand, and finally, the people or organizations to which much non-core work is outsourced. Arguably, at the level of industries, transition to this form of spider's web may denote the emergence of a 'dynamic network' or 'flexible specialization'. Here, great numbers of small independent units may co-ordinate information about market needs, designs and so on, with each unit performing a specific activity which corresponds to that unit's core capability or expertise, and with the whole benefiting from the specialization, motivation and flexibility of the parts (particularly when compared to the conduct of similar activities within the framework of the large vertically integrated organization).

Of the wider network form of the spider's web, the shamrock, Rank Xerox in the UK is quoted as illustrative. In particular, the firm's use of part-time and temporary full-time workers to cope with surges or dips in demand, precludes the need for a more substantial group of permanent employees than might otherwise be the case. Quinn cites Xerox's employment of seventy former employees as full-time but temporary contractors to which work from its central office is outsourced. More broadly still, Quinn's description of 'shamrock' industries invokes a network metaphor. He is not alone in describing Nike's complex of outsourcing relationships, which permits Nike to concentrate on value-adding activities such as research and development and marketing, whilst others specialize in production. In Figure 7.3 the links between Nike and its first-tier and second-tier subcontractors are portrayed. (The diagram is a simplification of an analysis by Donaghu and Barff [1990] of Nike's strategic and spatial development which for Dickens illustrates the dynamic network/flexibly specialized form of organization.) Nike acts as a co-ordinator of production activities. Its relationships with the first-tier partners in the network pertain to the manufacture of either 'niche' products in Nike's range of athletic sportswear (i.e. with 'developed partners'), or more standardized goods which sell in large volume. (Another strand of first-tier relationships is concerned with the development of future 'developed partners'.) Second-tier subcontractors specialize in the supply of materials and components in support of production within the first tier. In Quinn's view the partners in such a network specialize in the value chain activities in which they are strongest (or 'world class') and the co-ordination task is one of managing the individual knowledge bases in a synergistic way. (Ironically, as this manuscript was being completed, Nike issued a warning concerning its revenues and profits for the quarter ending 31 May, 1997. It cited the 'one-off' costs of a factory closure and an increase in the cancellation of orders by US retailers as contributory factors to the downturn in its fortunes [*Financial Times*, 1997a: 19].)

Of course the term 'flexible specialization' is most closely associated with the work of Piore and Sabel (1984). They argue that there has been an 'industrial divide' between forms of organizing associated with mass consumption/mass production, and those which underpin an emerging form, namely flexible specialization. This term refers to the capacity of a production process to respond efficiently to changes in demand for customized products. As suggested above, such a process has for its constituents numbers of relatively small firms co-ordinated by a 'hub' organization.

The Italian textile industry in the Prato district is central to Piore and Sabel's enunciation of their argument. In Prato, successes in export and employment, over a fifteen-year period to 1982, are partly explained by reference to the development of increasingly sophisticated production technology. In addition, they trace the historical trend towards fragmentation of the sector, as large integrated mills gave way to small units specializing

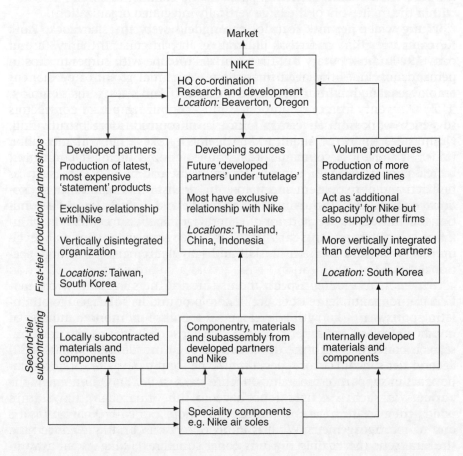

Figure 7.3 Links between Nike and its subcontractors. *Source*: Dicken (1992) (based on Donaghu and Barff 1990), reprinted with permission from Paul Chapman Publishing Limited, London.

in different stages in production. The 'hub' firm (known as the *impannatore*) focuses upon the creation of new fashion designs, while encouraging others to experiment either with new materials or production processes, according to their specialism. (The example of Benetton is often mentioned in this regard.) Moving away from Prato, the notion of flexible specialization, or 'flexi spec', has been the subject of much contested debate, particularly as regards the extent to which it signifies a more general decline of the Fordist paradigm of mass production. Moreover, a key issue of the debate relates to evidence of, and the prospects for, greater decentralization of industry, as large corporations downsize and the small independent firm attains a greater significance. This issue also embraces hopes for a revival in the craft tradition of work, linked to the reskilling of work and prospects of more autonomy for employees.

DOWNSIZING, DELAYERING AND EMPOWERMENT

Contrary to the promise that downsizing and delayering seemed to hold for companies that undertook radical restructuring during the 1980s and early 1990s, recent years have brought renewed fears of corporate under-performance. The popular business literature is replete with new slogans for and explanations of the difficulties currently bedevilling organizations. 'Hollowing out', 'corporate amnesia', and 'dumbsizing' are all expressions suggestive of possible adverse implications of organizational restructuring. Noting a survey by the American Management Association that found that under half of those companies that had downsized since 1990 achieved increased operating profits in subsequent years, an article in *The Economist* points to the risk of memory loss in downsized organizations (*The Economist*, 1996a). Whilst not all memory loss is bad (and IBM and General Motors are quoted for their previous inability to 'forget' main-frame computers and 'gas-guzzling' cars), large-scale redundancies may be indicative of the expulsion of skill and knowledge, sources of organizational capability.

One very interesting aspect of this, bearing in mind the stress that Nonaka, for example, places upon the role of middle managers in stimulating processes of knowledge creation, is the disproportionate number of middle managers and supervisors who have lost their jobs due to downsizing compared to other employee groups in the United States. Middle managers, for instance, comprise less than 10 per cent of the US workforce but have suffered 17 per cent of the job losses since 1990. This phenomenon is at odds with a view of middle managers as 'the synapses within a firm's brain', co-ordinating the knowledge of the shop floor with the work of line and senior management. What is more, one point of critique concerning the emergence of flexible organizational structures addresses the way in which firms that have retreated to their core business and downsized out-source or subcontract work to ex-employees (Starkey *et al.*, 1991).

Recently the buzzword has become 'upsizing'. Reservations have been expressed by politicians in both of the last UK and US general elections campaigns about the social consequences of mass lay-offs and fears about the increasing reliance of families on part-time, temporary, insecure work. Within work organizations, upsizing has been adopted as the new rhetoric, partly as a consequence of the changing political debate but more directly because of a recognition that attention to customer service may have been harmed. For example, in April 1996 the US regional telephone company, Nynex, was ordered by the New York Public Services Commission to pay a rebate of $50 million to its customers due to a decline in service standards. And, in Britain, one of the recently established private regional railway companies, South-West Trains, was threatened with a fine of £1 million (having already paid £900,000 in penalties) after leaving itself with too few drivers to meet its franchise performance targets, and cancelling a large number of trains during February and March 1997. Services were restored to acceptable levels in April 1997 (*Financial Times*, 1997b).

However, there are reservations about upsizing, too. One of these is that, as with downsizing and delayering, upsizing is merely another of those management fads. Nohria holds the view that upsizing represents an attempt by some firms to correct the adverse publicity associated with downsizing that has been damaging to corporate image and related customer loyalty. This stands in contrast to another position on the issue of upsizing. This alternative view has it that firms such as IBM and AT&T, which cut their staff dramatically only a few years ago but in 1996 announced plans to hire in significant numbers (e.g. 10,000 employees in IBM's computer services business), are doing so having refocused and with specific new skills and competences in mind (*The Economist*, 1996b). It is too early to be conclusive about which of these is the more convincing explanation of upsizing. Moreover, it needs to be recognized that whether or not the labels 'downsizing' or 'delayering' continue to be applied, and whether or not the practice is 'strategically' driven or more short term in orientation, the phenomenon of seeking cost savings through shrinkage of staff numbers is far from dead. Comments about the prevalence of short-term horizons in US and UK industry and the role played in this by relationships between British firms and City financial institutions are not uncommon (Hayes and Garvin, 1982; Williams *et al.*, 1983). Hence the wider pressures that may be at work and influential upon major restructuring decisions are suggested.

On the subject of empowerment Rosabeth Moss Kanter (1983) portrays the 'upside' of organizational restructuring and the promotion of corporate entrepreneurship. It reveals a positive view of the empowerment of subordinate employees taken within the type of organization that Kanter considers to be 'change masters'. In a manner bearing a striking resemblance to Quinn's (1980) description of processes of logical incrementalism, Kanter characterizes ways in which the commitment of employees to organizational objectives is elicited as they become more greatly empowered. The processes involved refer to the coalition-building, negotiation and bargaining that are employed by members of an organization to acquire the information and resources they need to get their work done. Further, Kanter says, such processes serve as a check against the possible abuse of power of others within the firm. For Kanter, achieving local access to resources is exemplified by the development of formal mechanisms operating outside the organizational hierarchy, such as 3M's 'innovation banks', or the steering committees within divisions of Honeywell which regularly solicited ideas for the formation of their problem-solving task teams.

A rather different view is to be found in some of the literature on contemporary developments in human resource management, where a critical perspective of the rhetoric of restructuring, empowerment and the development of a climate of trust within organizations is adopted. Instead of a portrait of such practices as enabling a liberating quality of working life, the imagery is of surveillance and control, whether by management of subordinates directly, through electronic means, or via employees within their own peer groups. Such an approach brings into question the extent to which emerging (and so-called 'HRM') employee management practices owe their implementation to strategic considerations, or to the nurturing of learning individuals within learning organizations.

For Sewell and Wilkinson, for example, the emulation of Japanese-style human resource management in British organizations has served merely to give the impression of lessening management control and ceding authority to more autonomous employees whilst actually strengthening the hand of senior management. Processes of socialization that are, in Ouchi's (1980) work, associated with the building of core, shared organizational values with which individual employees identify and work together towards achieving, may be understood somewhat differently. Rather, personnel selection and appraisal methods may be seen as constraining the development and pursuit of alternative interests. Further, 'devolutionism' occurs, whereby centralization and delegation simultaneously allow senior management to have increased control over work and information, without the necessity for pre-existing levels of hierarchy (Sewell and Wilkinson, 1992).

The Japanese-owned UK plant of Kay Electronics studied by Sewell and Wilkinson illustrates their argument; it appears to match the 'ideal type' of manufacturer (of mass market consumer electronics) but closer inspection reveals that there is more to the implementation of contemporary work and organization practices there than first meets the eye. The ingredients are all there: a flatter organizational structure than hitherto; the wide use of team-based working; and the enthusiasm of senior managers for extending the autonomy of shop-floor workers (or 'members' as they became known). However, to this mix is added quite different flavours. At Kay, managers did not rely upon the goodwill or commitment of employees to ensure that standards for maintaining quality, for example, were met. So, in the assembly of the printed circuit boards that were the key value activity of the plant, a 'traffic light' system for monitoring quality was set up. This involved red, amber and green cards being allocated to the work of different work groups, depending on the quantity and quality of work produced by these groups, and information from visual and electronic forms of inspection devised by production specialists at Kay's Japanese headquarters. These cards were displayed visually, being suspended above the heads of the teams of workers from the superstructure of the production line. Such a display serves as a mechanism for alerting individual employees of the need to maintain or improve upon performance but also conveys the required message to the work team as a whole, in doing so allowing for a peer-group form of surveillance. When considered alongside the details of employee performance, absenteeism and so on, stored electronically at the plant, the picture that is built up of employee management at Kay Electronics seems a long way removed from the rhetoric of empowering workers through new HRM practices (Sewell and Wilkinson, 1992).

SKUNKWORKS, SHAMROCKS AND NETWORK ORGANIZATIONS

In this section, more of the problems and opportunities associated with organizational restructuring are considered. First, the implementation of matrix or other mechanisms for promoting teamwork within organizations forms the topic for discussion. Later in the section, core-periphery labour, outsourcing and strategic networks/flexible specialization issues will be addressed, as referred to by Quinn's 'shamrocks' notion.

An interesting place to start is with an insight into the difficulties of change that might be experienced in attempting to develop a team-oriented approach within a large organization. A study of product development at Ford of Europe (Starkey and McKinlay, 1996) tells a story of interfunctional rivalry and the low historical status of study teams, factors which jointly contribute to impede a co-operative approach to an essential activity. 'Traditional' product development at Ford Europe is described as being dominated by a centralized research and development function, and somewhat remote from customer requirements, such that the design engineers 'wouldn't know a customer if they tripped over one' (Starkey and McKinlay, 1996: 216). Moreover, the product development process was divorced from the rest of the firm's operations and the 'bean counters' (i.e. people in the finance function) held sway when it came to the vital investment decisions, with considerations of cost tending to outweigh those of product quality. Attempting to remedy the situation initially took the form of a proposal from the product development function to move towards matrix management, by setting up product development 'programme teams' involving representatives from vehicle design, planning and finance functions. This followed a report which contrasted the 'environment of harmony' identified at competitors such as Mazda with the 'environment of competition' characteristic of Ford of Europe and aimed at increasing teamwork and customer focus. Significantly, for a company where restructuring was understood as the routine response to any crisis, the challenge now was to stop 'thinking structurally' and to see the move to matrix management across the company as a whole as a genuine change in its way of doing things.

A number of problems of change were to surface before a more widespread move towards matrix management could be established at Ford of Europe. Most critical among these was opposition from the manufacturing function, which was an expression of not only 'not invented here' syndrome but the fact that it was a move sponsored from within the product development function. (In passing, it should be noted that other problems centred around the locus of authority or split loyalties between the programme team and the 'home' function of the employees involved.) Ironically, another opportunity for considering matrix management throughout Ford of Europe was occasioned in 1989, when a study led by the vice-president for manufacturing was undertaken, with a key strategic consideration being how to drastically reduce product development 'cycle time' (by eighteen months). This 'simultaneous engineering' study, as it was known, looked again to Japan for exemplars of good product development practice, and in particular at Honda, Toyota and Mazda, where programme management had diffused throughout the company by 1979. Aspects of these firms' collective approach, including the use of temporary cross-functional teams, were seen as capable of being emulated by Ford of Europe. The study recommended the extension of programme management to cover additionally the marketing, manufacturing and supply functions. The role of programme managers was primarily to keep open channels of communication between functional representatives and to build an early consensus among the participants regarding product and technological objectives. To these ends programme managers were able to gain access to the vice-president as a last resort.

Delbridge and Turnbull (1992) cite the structure and organization of work teams and the interpersonal relations that develop within them as being crucial to securing employee commitment to the task in hand and to wider organizational objectives. Delbridge and Turnbull illustrate this with reference to UK truck manufacturer Iveco-Ford and their introduction, in 1989, of a new supervisory structure in place of the old foreman arrangement. Here, an attempt by management to 'tap into' the detailed operational knowledge of employees on the shop floor included the introduction of a new 'Co-ordinator' position. The function of Co-ordinators is cited as being

> to bridge the role of foreman and hourly-paid operatives, with each Co-ordinator (team leader) responsible for volume, quality, minor maintenance, operator training, process checks, allocating jobs at the start of each shift and reporting on lateness, sickness and absenteeism. Team leaders become the 'eyes and ears of management on the

shopfloor and provide a direct means of communication with the workforce. The aim is to keep the teams small ... so that they develop their own identity and pull together to solve problems – management's problems.

(Delbridge and Turnbull, 1992: 62–3)

This example of a team-based approach may be said to reflect a 'hard' form of human resource management, being concerned with the maximization of the use of human resources and less to do with the improvement of employee capabilities and autonomy implied in a 'soft' type of HRM. A more positive example of team-working can be given, however both with reference to lower- and higher-order employees. Research into organizational changes associated with the introduction of computer-integrated technologies has noted the development of team working in conjunction with changes in employee responsibility, reward and supervision (Bessant, 1993).

Bessant's study looked at the 'successful' implementation of computer-integrated technologies in twenty-eight manufacturing organizations between 1988 and 1990. Among the chief features associated with changes in work organization that have accompanied and facilitated the introduction of the new technology was the establishment of multiskilled, autonomous operator teams. A number of variations on the theme are described by Bessant, including quality circles, task forces, multidisciplinary teams and cross-functional teams. 'Significant' increases in employee responsibility through greater autonomy are reported, and this together with operator flexibility, is seen as key to realizing the skills and potential of the workforce. In addition, changes in the reward system were commonly viewed as being of 'high priority' for achieving the new work structures. In particular, findings from the Bessant study highlight shifts in the basis of payment from 'output achieved' to payment for 'skills and quality'. The role of the new type of reward system is described as 'the bedrock on which the attainment of extra flexibility rests' (Bessant, 1993: 200). Changes in the role of supervision were also identified as being critical. In most cases, sample companies provided evidence of a shift in supervisory role which permitted the level of responsibility to be shifted down to the operators in order to allow them to do what they saw as necessary to perform the job. This shift was seen as reflective of a fundamental change in the managerial approach to employee relations, from one emphasizing monitoring and control of the labour force to a more supportive and collaborative role.

In recent years much has been made of the need for increasingly flexible labour strategies, and successive Conservative governments in Britain have boasted of the superior flexibility of the British labour market and the advantages to competitiveness for British firms that this has brought. Indeed, this last sentence was written on the day after the Policy Studies Institute published a report on changing employment practices in Britain (Casey *et al.*, 1997a). This identified that half of all employees were working variable hours every week, double the amount doing so in the mid-1980s. The common use of variable hours applied across sectors of the economy and related to both blue-collar and white-collar workers. However, the more interesting finding was of the less than dramatic use of other forms of flexible labour such as short-term contracts or subcontracting. In both manufacturing and services only 4 per cent of workplaces were 'high users' of such practices (i.e. over 5 per cent of the workforce were on short-term or other flexible contracts), though in the public sector nearly half of schools, for example, were high users. The claim that employers are using flexible employment strategies does not find favour:

> There has been much talk about the growth of exotic forms of flexibility – temporary and zero hours contracts and sub-contracting – but the real change hasn't been here. What has changed is at the margins – employers need a few more hours here or there, and employees give this, sometimes for pay, sometimes not, and sometimes for matching time off. Such flexibility is vitally important to business success but it goes largely unsung.
>
> *(Casey, et al., 1997b: n.p.)*

Further, whilst

> We have been repeatedly told that employees' need for job security has to be sacrificed in the interest of competitiveness ... This study shows this is rarely necessary. Employers have choices: some can smooth fluctuations in production and maintain permanent employment with regular hours, most others can produce efficiently by combining full-time and part-time work with small variations in hours. Few need to turn to temporary working or to major fluctuations in hours – and in pay – to be competitive. Job income and security is rarely incompatible with business efficiency.
>
> *(Casey et al., 1997b: n.p.)*

If the above makes a dent in the idea that employers have been moving radically or strategically towards the employment of peripheral 'buffer' labour, the 'endangered core' thesis opposes the view of the autonomy of the permanent staff in organizations. Whittington (1990; 1991), for example, analyses the management of professional research and development workers. The traditional values of professional scientists working within R&D have celebrated specialized expertise and the autonomy of staff has enabled them to identify with technical priorities which were not necessarily congruent with wider organizational goals and objectives. Whittington's study of six in-house R&D units within large manufacturing firms and eight independent contract research organizations explains an emerging pattern of externalization of research and development work. Formerly centralized (and centrally funded) R&D activity is being transferred either to separate divisional profit centres within the firm or to external subcontractors and consultants, in order to elicit a greater degree of market, rather than bureaucratic, control. The general argument is that the effect of this development has been to expose R&D work (and workers) to the discipline of the market whilst enhancing the managerial control over R&D required to realize more efficient innovation (Whittington, 1991).

The description, above, of the shamrock form of organization identified by Quinn recalls a set of connected debates about the emergence (or not) of flexible labour policies, flexible specialization and network-based organization. More broadly, the extent to which such practices and forms have become established may be reflective of the transition towards post-Fordist modes of organization. This is not the place to attempt to be exhaustive about reviewing these debates though some connected points having particular relevance to this volume may be outlined. In general, the common themes of these discussions revolve around the content of change (if any) and how radical a break there has been with the practices and forms of the past, Fordist, era. This has been referred to as the 'search for discontinuities' (Hyman, 1991: 261). Less prevalent are treatments of contemporary phenomena which place developments at the organizational level in the context of wider societal and economic ones, or which look to the past for inspiration and explanation, as well as to the here and the now. It is worth summarizing some of Hyman's comments at this juncture.

Hyman points to a certain nostalgia and romanticism inherent in arguments for flexible specialization and like concepts. For example, there is an alternative way to construe the debatable increased significance of self-employment or small firms to the enterprise economy. So, rather than see this as integral to new competition, based upon the co-ordination of the activities of disparate specialized firms, one may understand the development in terms of the lack of other available opportunities, within a context of high unemployment. Further, the vulnerable nature of such employment and the extent to which such workers or enterprises are the subject of 'a subordinate relationship with large-scale capital' needs to be recognized (Hyman, 1991: 260). In addition, an equally unfavourable position contends that whilst

> there is little doubt that ... new industrial spaces have emerged ... they have been given both exaggerated importance by their proponents and also explained in excessively uniform terms, given their great diversity ... We are seeing increasing tendencies towards internationalization and the global integration of local and national economies. Regional and local economies have to be understood in the context of the global field ... Discussion of entrepreneurial artisans and of disintegrating and localizing corporations should not blind us to the growing power and influence of global industrial and finance capital. Multinational corporations are ... the real shakers and shapers of the world economy ... The multinational corporation remains the most powerful agent of the restructuring process ... What is at work is

not corporate fragmentation but, in fact, more effective corporate integration.

(Amin and Robins, 1990: 7–34)

As this and the previous chapter have already illustrated, the adoption of advanced technology and novel production concepts do not necessarily translate on implementation into non-Fordist or anti-Tayloristic approaches to organization. Arguably, proponents of flexible specialization, or of intelligent enterprises for that matter, underplay the potential 'downside' of the implementation of new processes. One could argue that bidding to resolve the 'productivity dilemma' has little necessarily to do with increasing employee autonomy or multiskilling. Hyman indicates that in high-technology sectors the flexibilization thesis may hold greater persuasion than in traditional manufacturing. However, as Sewell and Wilkinson's study of Kay Electronics demonstrates, the implementation of new production concepts may be accompanied by patterns of control and surveillance bearing closer resemblance to neo-Fordist/neo-Taylorist concepts than to post-Fordist or post-Tayloristic ones.

Pertinent to the previous point, Hyman warns against taking a range of concepts for granted. With regard to the labels Fordism, post-Fordism and neo-Fordism, for example, care should be exercised concerning the subject of explanation. Is it radical (or not so radical) change within the workplace? Or much wider change taking in connected developments, nationally and internationally, in product markets, technology, and *laissez-faire* macro-economic policy? Perhaps the labels are being applied too glibly; maybe there are limits, temporal and of degree, to which work organization in Britain as a whole, say, has ever been 'Fordist' (Hyman, 1991: 275).

Similarly, as referred to above, the distinction between 'core' (and thus skilled, flexible employees) and 'peripheral' (and thus narrowly skilled, inflexible employees) is all too neatly drawn, and represents 'a gross over-simplification' (Hyman, 1991: 259–60). Thus whilst not wishing to undervalue the changes that do appear to have taken place related to organizational restructuring and interfirm relations, it is wise to avoid exaggerating these by the invocation of 'grandiose' terms and categories.

Finally, on the subject of flexibility *per se*, one has to come to terms first with the ambiguity with which the term is employed, as has already been recognized in Chapter 4. In addition, there is an ideology of flexibility, to be considered alongside structural and institutional aspects of the notion. Here, the appeal of flexible specialization and the flexible firm concepts may be understood 'more as a rhetorical slogan than as an analytical instrument' (Hyman, 1991: 281). In this rhetoric 'flexible' or 'flexibility' are imbued with goodness whereas 'rigidities', such as job security or employment rights for part-time employees, invariably are seen as 'bad'.

SUMMARY

Recognizing the ideological dimension to restructuring and flexibility draws attention to the matter of what interests are served by changes in existing practices and what distributions of power are expressed in the adoption and realization of new processes. This is linked to the question of who wins and who loses from organizational change. However, care needs to be exercised so that the issue of flexibility does not become seen as merely a matter of ideology. 'Structural' changes, external and internal, to organizations have been occurring to which the term 'crisis of capitalism' has been applied. Such developments may be seen in the light of a concept of 'historical disjuncture' as represented by the contrast between the relative period of stability and economic growth following the Second World War and contemporary uncertainties and instability. In responding to and preparing for the 'certainty of uncertainty' with which this particular historical disjuncture is associated, notions of flexibility have taken on new significance. However, the specific choices that governments and organizations make are the product of prevailing arrangements, traditions, interests and understandings regarding the rigidities to be maintained and those to be abandoned (Hyman, 1991). Recognizing this may enable a resolution of the voluntarism–determinism debate. Further discussion of this and of the role of ideology and power within processes of managing change form the substance of the final chapter of this book, within a consideration of the leadership of change.

LEADERSHIP AND ORGANIZATIONAL CHANGE

8

INTRODUCTION

In this final chapter the topic is the leadership of change. In general, leadership has been one of the most popular areas of research within organizational and management studies. The issue of the possible links that there may be between leadership, strategic change and organizational performance is one which occurs time and again in the strategy literature. But it is acknowledged that perhaps more heat than light has been generated on the subject of the difference, if any, that leaders make to organizations and on the role of leadership in the management of change.

Within this literature there has been a preoccupation with the personality traits and behavioural characteristics of individual leaders. Over recent decades research on leadership traits has attempted to isolate the characteristics of leaders as distinguished from non-leaders and successful versus unsuccessful leaders. A wide variety of traits has been examined and studies have commonly singled out factors such as intelligence, initiative and self-assurance, *inter alia*, as definitive of successful leaders. Trait theory research declined in the face of the rather obvious limitations associated with the genre, such as the impossibility of mere mortals living up to the myriad ideal leadership characteristics proposed. Or, that because of the range of backgrounds, experiences, organizational conditions encountered, timing and serendipity, there may be a good many exceptions to the rule concerning the characteristics of successful individual leaders. Moreover, underlying this thinking is a view of an élite 'officer corps' of managers who possess the necessary characteristics of leaders. Arguably, the trait theories associated with past research in psychology and organizational behaviour have retained a certain pervasiveness. For example, one might consider the inherent assumptions about requisite personal characteristics which drive the selection criteria and recruitment methods of organizations seeking to fill managerial staff positions.

Where trait theory research emphasized the primacy of the individual over situational contingencies, a second stream of leadership research has sought to take into account these wider considerations. This branch of the literature includes style and contingency theories of leadership. Style theories tend to be based on the assumption that the employment of particular styles of leadership by managers will have varying effects on the motivation and effectiveness of employees. Styles are often depicted in such a way as to enable some attempted comparison of their effectiveness, typically along authoritarian and democratic dimensions. Invariably, these dimensions are differentiated according to the locus of power over decision-making throughout the organization, or the kinds of control and communication processes employed within it. Undergraduates on management studies degrees become familiar very quickly with the translation of these dimensions into alternative leadership and management styles (McGregor's Theory X and Theory Y, Likert's system 1 [exploitative authoritative] and system 4 [participative group management], for example).

Contingency theorists try to cater for variables related to the position of leaders within a work group or take into account the task that is being performed. Such an approach is exemplified by the work of Fiedler, who focused on the relationship between leader and work group, and the structure of the task to be performed, as determinants of the most effective style of leadership. Considering the contribution of research on leadership as a whole, Pettigrew and Whipp (1991) lament that 'leadership ... has proved to be one of the most appealing and yet intractable subjects within management'. Pettigrew and Whipp (1991) cite four principal limitations affecting our understanding of the nature and contribution of leaders and leadership to organizational effectiveness over time. These are:

1. A tendency to conceive of leadership from a command-obey-control perspective.
2. The emphasis of some of the popular business literature (as written by academics, consultants and practitioners alike) on simple prescriptions for effective leadership, based on stories of heroic, visionary leaders in highly specific situations.
3. Ignorance of interactions between context and strategic decision-making and the role of leaders within processes of strategy development and change.
4. A propensity to assume rather than to more sharply and carefully analyse what difference leadership makes to organizational effectiveness.

By contrast, one might consider that the literature on the leadership of change has somewhat neglected the temporal, continuing nature of organizational life, and the interrelationship between the organization under scrutiny and the wider context of competition and so on. In addition, the idea of collective leadership, which characterizes leading change as an activity which is not so reliant on one specific individual, has been relatively underemphasized. Having begun by outlining the range of approaches towards understanding leadership, the chapter proceeds by presenting Tom Peters's view of the leadership of change to illustrate the manner in which contemporary popular management writing deals with of the topic. Subsequently, Pettigrew's study of Peugeot Talbot will serve to exemplify a processual and contextually sensitive alternative approach to understanding leadership and change. Finally, the chapter reconsiders the issue of leadership in terms of the debate between voluntaristic and deterministic approaches to understanding change, and in the relationship between leadership, the promotion of 'strong' culture and organizational effectiveness.

PETERS ON CHIEF EXECUTIVES

The work of Tom Peters represents a commonly found view of the nature of leadership and the contribution of individual leaders to the management of change. One of the central aspects of his view of leadership is that one can learn from the exploits of individual chief executives who have led successful organizations. Another key aspect of this view concerns the ingredients which combine to promote organizational excellence and success through leadership. In a sense, these may be said to constitute a 'nuts and bolts' view of a technique of leadership. The critical factors to leadership and success are cited in *A Passion for Excellence* (Peters and Austin, 1985) and include the following:

- passion
- care
- intensity
- attention
- drama
- implicit/explicit use of symbols.

More concisely, the essence of leadership as learned from successful individuals such as Bill Hewlett (Hewlett-Packard), Steve Jobs (Apple Computer) and Jan Carlzon (Scandinavian Air System) seems to revolve around 'love' and 'vision'. Hence Peters relates the reply of one chief executive to a question posed at Harvard Business School about the secret of success at their company (the Trammell Crow real estate organization). This was indeed 'love'. 'Love' equals intense and passionate caring about the organization in question and its products. Such love extends apparently even to the most mundane products and services, including hamburgers, cookies and garbage collection, as Peters notes.

As far as vision is concerned, this is stated as representing a concise statement or picture of where the organization is heading and why its employees should be proud of it. Attention, use of symbols and drama are the building blocks of leadership which contribute to such vision but also to the detailed realization of such ideals. Moreover, in Peters's view, vision is neither amenable to planning nor a collective activity. Thus any written statement of vision merely expresses previously implicit values about the mission and direction of the organization. In addition, it is stated that: 'A vision must always start with a single individual. We are wary ... of "committee visions" ... The raw material of the effective vision is invariably the result of one man's or woman's soul-searching' (Peters and Austin, 1985: 266). So, although there needs to be a major team effort to buy into this vision, Peters sees the individual leader as a 'shockingly powerful' central figure.

The practical implications for strategic change that flow from this view of Peters are reported as follows:

1. Change is first a matter of *quantity* of attention to the particular issue at hand, not so much the *quality* of attention paid to that issue (that comes later). Thus in implementing a quality improvement programme, say, it is important to stimulate conversation about it throughout the firm, it is a matter of getting the ball rolling, to let everyone know that quality is an issue, even if the details of execution remain vague.

2. There is an important role for the strategic leader in the management of symbols through drama. Here, the example of Jack Welch on assuming the chair of General Electric (GE) in 1981 is offered by Peters. In short, one of Welch's first acts was to dismantle much of the strategic planning function, which had played a major role in the development of strategic thinking within the firm (and indeed the subject of strategic management) over the previous decade or so. The activity of strategic development was thus sent back to the strategic business units at GE in a highly symbolic and dramatic move.

3. Language is fundamental and so, more specifically, is a 'language of attention'. Where Peters considers the use of 'cast' or 'crew members' at Disney or McDonalds, presumably one might also consider the substitution of 'customers' for 'passengers' or 'clients' in terms of the symbolic significance of individual words in organizations seeking to reshape former missions or images. The role of stories and their impact on changing organizations is seen as crucial. Thus Peters declares that: 'the new or modified [strategic] thrust is not credible until there is a tapestry of legends to support it' (Peters and Austin, 1985:281). So, once leaders recognize the significance of story-telling, they can consider themselves as 'story-trail creators'. What is more, it does not matter if the stories are not actually true. For example, take the story of McDonald's chief Ray Kroc and a franchise in Winnipeg. Here, a fly was found, in contravention of McDonald's Quality, Service, Cleanliness, and Value mission statement. The story goes that within two weeks the Winnipeg franchisee lost the franchise because of this. Perhaps. Perhaps not. But the point is that the story spread like wildfire and the idea that Ray Kroc could have done something like this was credible and symbolized McDonald's strategy to such an extent that 'after this story made the rounds a whole lot of McDonald's people found nearly mystical ways to eliminate flies ... from their shops' (Peters and Austin, 1985: 278).

Whether legendary or not, the actions of leaders are considered by Schein (1985) to be fundamental to the formation, transformation and destruction of culture through various stages of the organizational life cycle. Indeed, he suggests, rather than to focus on the personal traits and styles of good leaders, understanding leadership is simpler if it is accepted that 'the unique and essential function of leadership is manipulation of culture' (Schein, 1985: 317). As with Peters, Schein asserts the critical role in 'culture creation' of the individual founder-leader having vision and the means to articulate and to enforce that vision. In what Schein refers to as organizational mid-life, the task for the leader of an organization which has already developed 'a substantial history of its own' will vary according to the path of that development. So, an organization may have an 'integrated culture' despite having diversified product markets, or have diverse cultures as well as business units. Whatever the case: 'What the leader most needs is insight into the ways in which culture can aid or hinder the fulfilment of the organization's mission and the intervention skills to make the desired changes happen' (Schein, 1985: 320). Recognizing that the individual founder-leader may be surrounded with like-minded senior colleagues who share this same vision, Schein remarks on the possibility that 'real changes' in direction may not occur in the absence of a sense that crisis threatens the very survival of the organization. With this in mind there may be, he says, a requirement for an external agent of change, able to break the 'tyranny of culture' in mature organizations. This, subject to the skills of the person involved, is a process of unfreezing, changing and then refreezing attitudes (cf. Lewin, 1951) which may be amenable to a planned approach to identifying barriers to change and then installing new values (Wilson, 1992).

A similar view of organizational development and leadership appears in work by Greiner (1994). Thus he cites five phases of evolutionary and revolutionary change in organizations as they grow and age. The evolutionary periods are distinguished by the principal guiding theme or preoccupation of management while the revolutionary periods are defined by the overriding problem (or 'crisis') facing management which needs to be solved if growth is to continue. For present purposes the details of the various phases are not necessary. What is of interest is that the first phase of Greiner's model specifies growth through creativity as its defining theme characterized by the technical or entrepreneurial acumen of an organization's founder, and founders are not considered to be especially gifted managers (or even interested in management). The latter point occasions the crisis of the first phase, which bears resemblance to the onset of 'mid-life' in Schein's framework. Here, the crisis is of leadership, and occurs with a need for 'strong business managers' who will be acceptable to the founder who, in turn, may have to step aside.

The remaining phases of Greiner's framework might be thought of further in terms of Schein's organizational life cycle concept. Hence successive periods of evolutionary growth (through direction by central management, delegation to subordinate employees, the use of formal systems of co-ordination, and the employment of more informal processes to encourage collaboration in teams) are accompanied by new revolutionary crises. The latter are crises of autonomy, then crises of control as senior management feel unable to manage the diversity that employee autonomy brings. Ironically, attempts to reassert control through improved co-ordination lead to a crisis of 'red tape'.

Intriguingly, Greiner considers many large US firms to be in the fifth phase of evolution, where growth through collaboration was the response to the previous crisis associated with red tape formality. The new 'crisis' then (Greiner speculates) is characterized by the need to manage the 'psychological saturation' of employees who grow exhausted by the intensity of teamwork and the constant pressure for innovation. Whilst not specifying the detail of the solution to this crisis, Greiner does suggest that this may involve developing structures and procedures which allow employees time to rest and to refresh (unfreeze?) their perspective. A final and interesting point is that Greiner complains about the lack of attention that the 'critical dimension of time' receives in management research and practices. However, in contrast to the discussion of a processual approach to understanding leadership of change which follows below, he wishes for historical approaches to analysing change which will enable managers to predict future problems. As in the work just described, this would be on the basis of previously identified, and typical, stages of evolution or revolution, whereas the forthcoming section attempts to present, arguably, a more rounded view of the interaction of leadership and leadership styles, contextual factors and organizational change over time.

LEADERSHIP: PROCESSES AND CONTEXT

An alternative view of leadership has been concerned to set organizational strategy and processes in context. In this view, in contrast to the above, the individual leader is accorded a rather restricted capacity to act, such is the nature of various external pressures impinging on organizational decision-making. Two strains of research are identifiable here. Their underlying predispositions mirror the distinction between competing versions of population ecology discussed in Chapter 1. The first of these is of a more severe and deterministic flavour than the second kind of thinking. In the first view, the environment reigns supreme. As with the pure strain of population ecology, objective external environmental conditions dictate the courses of action the organization is required to follow.

In the second view, there is a somewhat different conception of contexts, leaders and their contribution to strategic change and performance. As mentioned above, one might refer to the insights generated by the research of Andrew Pettigrew. In particular, the following observations have been made. First, that leadership is not well explained in terms of simple descriptions of the traits and behaviour of individual leaders. Second, that, in practice, the effective leading of change seems to be characterized by a number of factors. These include a combination of styles and practices over time. They also include a significant role for operational leaders at all levels of the organization (collective leadership), not just senior managers. Finally, there is a recognition of the interaction between what leaders do and the context in which they act. So behind the kind of 'macho' decision-making image that is often presented of leadership lies extensive preparation of the organization's strategic choices, together with the conditioning and legitimation required to enable these moves to be adopted and implemented.

Pettigrew refers to a number of 'primary conditioning devices', which involve the building of a climate of receptivity to change, building the capability to mount change, and the establishment of a change agenda regarding the future direction of the organization and related visions and values.

The case of Peugeot Talbot illustrates many of the themes referred to above. The Peugeot Talbot story may be divided into three broad periods of time each representing a phase with distinct strategy and leadership characteristics. The first period takes us from the inception of the Rootes car company group to about 1964. This was a phase where the Rootes family dominated the strategic direction of the firm. William Rootes had founded the firm and his sons Billy and Reginald assumed joint leadership until the outbreak of the Second World War. From then until the purchase of Rootes by Chrysler in 1964, other Rootes members held sway over the company, which during that time was failing to develop expertise in product planning, finance and training. Faced with this internal context of weakness (the Linwood car plant was operating at half-capacity and new ranges were suffering by comparison with those of Ford, BMC and Vauxhall), the new Chrysler management saw the need for a fundamental change in strategy. The remedy for the ills of the old Rootes company took the form of importing Chrysler managers from the United States together with some US-inspired managers from Ford UK, to manage a strategy of rapid expansion of production volume. It also involved the transfer of finance, accounting and operating procedures derived at Chrysler's home base in Detroit to what was now Chrysler UK. However, these changes were undermined partly by a failure to condition and prepare the UK subsidiary for such transformational change. This was not helped by suspicion of the motives of successive Managing Directors (Hunt 1967–73, Lander 1973–6, Lacey 1976–8) and functional directors. Such scepticism revolved around the apparent loyalty of senior management to the paymasters from Detroit as well as a feeling that they were exiles who were rejects from Chrysler Corporation's own débâcles in the 1960s. After several years of sustained, and often heavy, loss-making, and protracted negotiations over the underwriting of losses with the UK government, Chrysler Corporation sold its UK, French and Spanish operations to Peugeot SA, in 1978.

The story of Peugeot Talbot through the late 1970s and the 1980s is a rather different one from that of Chrysler. A degree of continuity has been associated with the regimes of Turnbull (Chief Executive between

1979–84) and Whalen (Assistant Managing Director from October 1981 and Managing Director from 1984). This continuity applied to the aim of rebuilding the firm's competitive base as a car manufacturer, with more modest aspirations regarding the scale of its operations. What has been a source of difference is the contrasting style of leadership which enabled transformational change at Peugeot Talbot. For Turnbull, this is said to have represented a combative style linked to his own vision of the requirements of international competition, with personal authority stemming from his own expertise in manufacturing. The combative element may be gleaned by his willingness to sit out a three-month strike in 1979, in order to send a message of new management–workforce relationships. So far this looks similar to the Peters approach to leadership of change. What should not be underestimated, however, is the extent to which Turnbull gave momentum to a change of attitudes within the firm which helped to create space for the developments that Whalen was later able to make. In short, Turnbull had facilitated the primary conditioning of the company, and its receptivity to change. His successor, Whalen, was then able to adopt a more consultative and relaxed approach in further developing the capacity for change. Such a sense of collective leadership was enhanced, for example, by the setting up of weekly meetings of an operations committee which helped to bring more open relations within senior management.

Where the work of Tom Peters may be considered as being illustrative of a strain of thinking in recent management writing which emphasizes the vision of individual leaders and their role in strategic choice and change, studies such as those of Pettigrew are more concerned to identify the collective and processual nature of leadership. In so doing they seek to address the contextual factors which affect (but do not determine) the range of actions available in different periods of an organization's history.

There has been much made throughout this and earlier chapters of this book of voluntaristic and deterministic perspectives of strategy and change. Leavy and Wilson (1994) consider the middle ground (labelled weak voluntarism/soft determinism throughout this text). This emerges from their study of leadership and change in four organizations based in the Republic of Ireland. In short, and similar to Pettigrew, a temporal and historical approach is invaluable in that:

> Long time-frames of analysis lend a perspective to the potency and powerlessness of individual action. They also re-emphasise the role of strategic choice. Leaders may be tenants of time and context but are rarely reduced to purely passive agents. They often can and do make their organisation's histories though not always in circumstances of their own choosing … the locus of influence over strategy formation varies over time between the organisation and its context, with some contexts being more structuring than others, but also with some leaders being better able to manage the requirements of contexts than others.
>
> *(Leavy and Wilson, 1994: 187–8)*

Three types of processes are specified which may help to explain possible interactions between context, leadership action and strategic change. These are social psychological, social exchange and cultural transmission (ideological) process. As described by Wilson and Leavy, social psychological processes of cognition condition the shared perceptions of people in organizations in such a way as to promote selective attention to environmental factors. Social exchange processes are presented as exemplified by theories of power-dependency in organizational analysis. Here, leaders embark on defensive strategic actions to protect their organizations from external threats. Cultural transmission processes are considered by Wilson and Leavy to explain the manner by which the values of leaders and their organizations reflect the internalization of a broader ideology emphasizing innovation and corporate growth.

One may object to the unidirectional nature of this categorization. For example, why should cultural transmission processes be invoked to explain the percolation of entrepreneurialism in Ireland (which Wilson and Leavy do with respect to Irish business leaders and firms responding to the 'national challenge' of the 1960s) but not be called upon to account for interactions between the wider culture, leadership and organizational ideology where such a risk-taking orientation is less highly valued? Setting aside this criticism, these processes do draw attention to symbolic, ideological and, most importantly, power-related aspects of leadership. If these are considered in terms of the nature of organizational learning (or lack of it) the interplay between leadership, organizational choice through time and the role of external contextual factors in influencing change may be highlighted.

A good place to start is with the loan of a book. In *Managing with Power* (1992) Jeffrey Pfeffer recounts the time he lent one of his other books on power in organizations (Pfeffer, 1981) to Tom Peters. Pfeffer notes the common assumption that the expression of power and conflict in organizations is 'bad' and necessarily impedes performance. Peters's act of scribbling 'not in effective organizations' in the margin of *Power in Organizations* where Pfeffer describes evidence of power and conflict exemplifies this brand of thinking. Somewhat caustically, Pfeffer then observes that Peters may have been right about the absence of power dynamics from his list of excellent companies, which he says could be a factor in why some of them were no longer excellent just a few years after the publication of Peters and Waterman's bestseller.

Despite the advice about 'simultaneous loose-tight properties' it will be remembered that a key thrust of *In Search of Excellence* concerned the significance of shared core values to competitiveness (Peters and Waterman, 1982). As chapters in both Part I and Part II of this book have demonstrated, this is but one example of the unitary perspective that runs through much of the literature on strategy and change. In common with some views about developing learning organizations, the assumption is that vision and the manipulation of key symbols in the building of culture is the leader's work. (Readers might like to consider this point in the light of the discussion of the work of Senge on the topic of learning as the leader's new work in Chapter 4). There is less attention, relatively speaking, to a number of other issues. These include the recognition of this activity as political with more than a little to do with the exercise of power. Further, the manifestation of subgoals or power-plays where a 'strong' leader exists, and the possibility that strong culture and unitary objectives may be predictors of inertia rather than organizational renewal tend to be ignored on this view.

The first of these points is borne out in a study by Eisenhardt and Bourgeois (1988) of leadership in small firms in the microcomputer industry. A key finding was that the existence of a strong, authoritarian chief executive promoted political manoeuvring amongst other senior managers. Thus under such conditions the latter would tend to engage in alliance and insurgency behaviours. The value of this conclusion is tempered somewhat by contemplation of another of the study's claims, concerning the nature of politics and power relations among participants in effective organizations. What Eisenhardt and Bourgeois do, in effect, is to retrace their steps towards a pluralistic view of organizational life, in favour of the more usual unitary view referred to at various stages in this volume. So, in a manner redolent of Peters and others on the subject, one finds that 'effective' organizations are characterized by the absence of (damaging) politics and conflicts of interest. Instead (and admittedly this is paring down the argument to the barest essentials) politicking among senior managers is analysed as both the source and outcome of poor organizational performance in firms where there are authoritarian chief executives.

Pfeffer makes a methodological point about the correlation of politics and poor performance, speculating on whether any such relationship is a direct one or should be better explained by reference to a correlation between politics and authoritarian management, where the latter is an intervening variable between politics and performance. He distinguishes between the environmental contingencies facing small high-tech companies of the type featured in Eisenhardt and Bourgeois's study and those of much larger organizations. Stereotypically, the small high-tech firm is presented as one operating in a fast-changing, competitive market in which the consequences of organizational and product innovation decisions quickly come home to roost. Authoritarian management (exemplified by a tendency of senior management to act in accordance with their own self-interest, rather than serve as agents for promoting the best interest of their organization) is less likely in this context, especially where senior executives are also major shareholders of the firm. Personal and organizational interest thus enjoy a happy coincidence and, intriguingly, compared to incrementalist thinking, what Pfeffer refers to as the distortions of organizational politics militate against high-quality decision-making.

What about the notion that the prevalence of strong central values, or a weak political environment, may be associated with inertia and the absence of fundamental change? The work of Danny Miller (1992) in *The Icarus Paradox* is again instructive on this point. Miller's research identifies four trajectories which characterize the path which formerly successful organizations follow into declining performance. Fundamentally, these trajectories (namely, 'focusing', 'venturing', 'inventing', and 'decoupling') represent one-time sources of success for organizations, providing the momentum to compete on the basis of certain key dimensions but eventually rigidifying these core values. In this way, Miller says, successful organizations become wedded to past strategies and blind to weaknesses or changes in competitive requirements. For example, Miller's study of Chrysler Corporation identifies the company's fluctuating fortunes in terms of the decoupling trajectory. The successes of Chrysler during Lynn Townsend's tenure as chief executive are described in terms of the development of the centrality of its marketing function and the pursuit of market share (as mentioned in Chapter 5, this needs to be seen in the context of Townsend's ambitions for the firm and its position *vis-à-vis* Ford and General Motors). These same factors are implicated in the downturn in Chrysler performance, as a preoccupation with 'bland' product proliferation and quarterly sales figures set in during the course of the 1970s and 1980s.

SUMMARY

As much as anything specific to the issue of the difference that leaders make to organizational performance and strategic change this chapter has served to illuminate the value of considering the interaction of contexts, processes and the content of change as this evolves over time. Such a view recognizes that what may be adjudged good leadership or organizational performance in one time period may not seem the same a few years down the line. Thus the adoption of a long time frame of analysis and a sensitivity to the context of leadership may enable the image under scrutiny (i.e. any need for and processes of managing fundamental change) to be brought into clearer focus. In addition, the sections above have contrasted the emphasis of some contributors to the topic upon individual leaders and their personal characteristics with that of those who define the collective nature of the leadership of change. Although it may be argued that the symbolic aspects of leadership are addressed within voluntaristic approaches such as that offered by Tom Peters, this tends to reflect a unitary view of organizations which underplays differences in and tensions between the values and goals of organizational constituents. Other less voluntaristic and particularly processual approaches are better reconciled to this diversity.

More broadly, this short volume has sought to identify the different preoccupations associated with voluntaristic and deterministic perspectives of change, or with the intermediate category of weak voluntarism/soft determinism. Generally, adherence to the central position of these perspectives would lead the practitioner or the researcher to different solutions to, or explanations of, the problem of change. From the perspective of voluntarism, the management of change is seen variously as amenable to being planned in advance, or as the preserve of the few, be it the individual chief executive or specialist planning departments. Radical shifts in strategic direction or structural arrangements tend to be emphasized, and at the popular end of writing on strategy and change especially, a unitary framework underpins the recommendations offered to practitioners. Issues of external context may receive a hearing, particularly in the conduct of exhaustive planning exercises, but are liable to be treated as 'objective' data rather than as contestable or open to interpretation. Hence there may be a focus on the attainment of strategic fit through the making of rational strategic choices about which markets to serve and the organization's basis of competition. Alternatively, attention to contextual factors may suffer in comparison to that which is accorded to episodic accounts of internal organizational affairs, from which recipes for achieving structural fit are distilled and generalized. Here, as various chapters have demonstrated, it is the role of individual leaders or senior managers to mould the commitment and values of employees in their organizations, partly through appropriate structural choices, which is seen as critical to the support of strategy. So, both wings of the voluntaristic perspective emphasize choice although differences exists in their treatment of the significance of planning, and in their preoccupation with external environmental or intra-organizational levels of analysis. Ironically, indeed paradoxically, those who concern themselves with questions of appropriate structural arrangements and internal processes from a voluntaristic perspective tend to offer such staunch prescriptions about restructuring that the advice takes on a deterministic 'one best way' quality. Less evangelistic research shows the degree to which supposedly outmoded structures and practices, or differences in organizing, persist.

Adhering to a deterministic perspective of change, by contrast, certainly puts environmental or technological contingencies, for example, to the fore. But the price that is paid is a dear one, in that human agency loses out to external constraint. Of course even in the most severe versions of such determinism, decisions regarding change remain in the hands of decision-makers. It is just that their zone of discretion is heavily constrained and their role limited, typically, to installing the 'correct' structure for their organization, according to the dictates of market uncertainty, the technology of production, and so on. Overall, where in the 1970s Child's article on strategic choice served to correct for the prevailing overemphasis on the deterministic nature of environmental forces (see Chapter 2), the value of population ecology or chaos theory applied to management in the 1990s and beyond is to temper an overoptimistic voluntarism.

The various approaches constituting what has been labelled here as weak voluntarism/soft determinism form a bridge between voluntaristic and deterministic perspectives. Drawing attention to various manifestations of the rhetoric of radical change, to the cognitive construction of 'the environment', or to the politics of learning or restructuring, these approaches qualify the extent of strategic choice by pointing to both internal and external factors which influence change. The preoccupation with fit mentioned above is replaced in (politically) incremental, interpretive or processual approaches by a concern with the emergent nature of strategy and change, and with characterizing fluctuating periods of 'drift' or 'fit' with subjective interpretations of environmental conditions. But unlike Senge, for example, the nature of such interpretation, and of organizational learning more generally, is located within an understanding of how the dominant coalition's view of the environment, or of the proper order of organizational values, dominates or is contested. In addition, the concepts of isomorphism, networks and organizational routines further draw attention to external and internal sources of change in the established practices of organizations, but also to potential difficulties in creating or diffusing new knowledge. To the extent that these, and other approaches presented in this book, address interactions between historical context, macro- and micro-level factors, and continuities and change in organizational practices, or tackle questions about the rhetoric and legitimacy of strategy and change, those interested in furthering their understanding of the management of change are well served.

REFERENCES

Abernathy, W.J. (1978) *The Productivity Dilemma: Roadblock to Innovation in the Automobile Industry*, Johns Hopkins University Press, Baltimore, MD, and London.

Abernathy, W.J., Clark, K. and Kantrow, A. (1981) The New Industrial Competition. *Harvard Business Review*, September–October, 69–81.

Aldrich, H.E. (1979) *Organizations and Environments*, Prentice-Hall, Englewood Cliffs, NJ.

Amin, A. and Robins, K. (1990) The Re-emergence of Regional Economies? The Mythical Geography of Flexible Accumulation. *Environment and Planning D: Society and Space*, **8**, 7–34.

Andrews, K. (1987) *The Concept of Corporate Strategy*, Richard D. Irwin, Chicago.

Ansoff, H.I. (1965) *Corporate Strategy: An Analytic Approach to Business Policy for Growth and Expansion*, McGraw-Hill, New York.

Ansoff, H.I. and McDonnell, E.J. (1990) *Implanting Strategic Management*, Prentice-Hall, Hemel Hempstead.

Bessant, J. (1985) The Integration Barrier: Problems in the Implementation of Advanced Manufacturing Technology. *Robotica*, **3**, 97–103.

Bessant, J. (1991) *Managing Advanced Manufacturing Technology*, Blackwell, Oxford.

Bessant, J. (1993) Towards Factory 2000: Designing Organizations for Computer-Integrated Technologies. In J. Clark (ed.) *Human Resource Management and Technical Change*, Sage, London.

Borum, F. (1990) Organizational Learning – Variants in Theory and Dilemmas in Practice. Revised version of paper prepared for Creativity and Innovation in Organizations at the Stanford Conference on Organizations, Asilomar, 22–24 April.

Burns, T. and Stalker, G.M. (1961) *The Management of Innovation*, Tavistock, London.

Casey, B., Metcalfe, H. and Millward, N. (1997a) *Employers Use of Flexible Labour*, Policy Studies Institute, London.

Casey, B., Metcalfe, H. and Millward, N. (1997b) Nine-to-Five Survives but in Name Only. Press release, 29 May.

Chandler, A. (1962) *Strategy and Structure*, MIT Press, Cambridge, MA.

Child, J. (1972) Organisational Structure, Environment and Performance: The Role of Strategic Choice. *Sociology*, **6**(1), 1–22.

Child, J. (1997) Strategic Choice in the Analysis of Action, Structure, Organizations and Environment: Retrospect and Prospect. *Organization Studies*, **18**(1), 43–72.

Clark, P.A. and Staunton, N. (1993) *Innovation in Technology and Organization*, Routledge, London.

Cohen, M.D., March, J.G. and Olsen, J.P. (1972) A Garbage Can Model of Organizational Choice. *Administrative Science Quarterly*, **17**, 1–25.

Cohen, S.S. and Zysman, M. (1994) The Myth of a Post-Industrial Economy. In E. Rhodes and D. Wield *Implementing New Technologies*, Blackwell, Oxford, 31–8.

Coopey, J. (1996) Crucial Gaps in 'the Learning Organisation': Power, Politics and Ideology. In K. Starkey (ed.) *How Organizations Learn*, International Thomson Business Press, London, 348–67.

Crosby, P. (1979) *Quality Is Free*, McGraw-Hill, New York.

Cyert, R.M. and March, J.G. (1963) *A Behavioural Theory of the Firm*, Prentice-Hall, Englewood Cliffs, NJ.

Delbridge, R. and Turnbull, P. (1992) Human Resource Maximization: The Management of Labour under Just-in-Time Manufacturing Systems. In P. Blyton and P. Turnbull *Reassessing Human Resource Management*, Sage, London.

Dicken, P. (1992) *Global Shift: The Internationalization of Economic Activity*, Paul Chapman, London.

DiMaggio, P.J. and Powell, W.W. (1991) The Iron Cage Revisited: Institutional Isomorphism and Collective Rationality in Organizational Fields. In W.W. Powell and P.J. DiMaggio *The New Institutionalism in Organizational Analysis*, University of Chicago Press, Chicago.

Donaghu, M.T. and Barff, R. (1990) Nike Just Did It: Subcontracting and Flexibility in Athletic Footwear Production. *Regional Studies*, **24**, 537–52.

The Economist (1996a) Fire and Forget. 20 April.

The Economist (1996b) And Now Upsizing. 8 June.

Eisenhardt, K. and Bourgeois, L. (1988) The Politics of Strategic Decision-making in High Velocity Environments: Towards a Mid-range Theory. *Academy of Management Journal*, **31**, 737–70.

Financial Times (1997a) Nike Warning Hits Sportsware. 30 May.

Financial Times (1997b) South-West Orders 30 New Trains. 14 May.

Faulkner, D. and Johnson, G. (eds) (1992) *The Challenge of Strategic Management*, Kogan Page, London.

Freeman, C. (1992) *The Economics of Hope*, Pinter, London.

Freeman, C. and Perez, C. (1994) Structural Crises of Adjustment, Business Cycles and Investment Behaviour. In E. Rhodes and D. Wield (eds) *Implementing new Technologies*, Blackwell, Oxford, 96–195.

Galbraith, J.R. and Kazanjian, R.K. (1986) *Strategy Implementation: Structure, Systems and Process*, West, New York.

Genus, A. (1995) *Flexible Strategic Management*, Chapman and Hall, London.

de Geus, A. (1996) Planning as Learning. In K. Starkey (ed.) *How Organizations Learn*, International Thomson Business Press, London, 92–99.

Goold, M. and Quinn, J.J. (1990) The Paradox of Strategic Controls. *Strategic Management Journal*, **11**(1), 43–57.

Greiner, L. (1994) Evolution and Revolution as Organizations Grow. In B. de Wit and R. Meyer (eds) *Strategy: Process, Content, Context*, West, Minneapolis/St Paul, 421–32.

Hamel, G. and Prahalad, C.K. (1993) Strategy as Stretch and Leverage. *Harvard Business Review*, March–April, 75–84.

Hammer, M. (1996) *Beyond Reengineering: How the Process-Centred Organization Is Changing our Lives*, HarperCollins, London.

Hammer, M. and Champy, J. (1993) *Reengineering the Corporation: A Manifesto for Business Revolution*, Nicholas Brealey, London.

Harrigan, K.R. (1985) *Strategic Flexibility*, Lexington Books, Lexington, MA.

Hax, A. (1994) Defining the Concept of Strategy. In B. de Wit and R. Meyer, *Strategy: Process, Content, Context*, West, Minneapolis/St Paul, 8–12.

Hayes, R. and Abernathy, W.J. (1980) Managing our Way to Industrial Decline. *Harvard Business Review*, July–August, 69–77.

Hayes, R. and Wheelwright, S.C. (1984) *Restoring our Competitive Edge*, Wiley, New York.

Hayes, R.H. and Garvin, D.A. (1982) Managing as if Tomorrow Mattered. *Harvard Business Review*, May–June, 265–73.

Hedlund, G. (1994) A Model of Knowledge Management and the N-form Corporation. *Strategic Management Journal*, **15**, special issue, 73–90.

Hill, S., Harris, M. and Martin, R. (1997) Flexible Technologies, Markets and the Firm: Strategic Choices and FMS. In I.P.M. McLoughlin and M. Harris *Innovation, Organizational Change and Technology*, International Thomson Business Press, London, 61–86.

Huff, A.S., Huff, J.O. and Thomas, H. (1992) Strategic Renewal and the Interaction of Stress and Inertia. *Strategic Management Journal*, **13**, 55–75.

Hyman, R. (1991) Plus ça Change? The Theory of Production and the Production of Theory. In A. Pollert (ed.) *Farewell to Flexibility?* Blackwell, Oxford, 259–83.

Jaques, E. (1990) In Praise of Hierarchy. *Harvard Business Review*, January–February, 127–33.

Jarillo, J.C. (1988) On Strategic Networks. *Strategic Management Journal*, **9**, 31–41.

Johnson, G. (1987) *Strategic Change and the Management Process*, Oxford, Blackwell.

Johnson, G. (1988) Rethinking Incrementalism. *Strategic Management Journal*, **9**, 75–91.

Kanter, R.M. (1983) *The Change Masters*, Unwin, London.

Kanter, R.M. (1989) *When Giants Learn to Dance*, Unwin, London.

Kay, N.M. (1992) Markets, False Hierarchies and the Evolution of the Modern Corporation. *Journal of Economic Behaviour and Organization*, **17**, 315–33.

Knights, D. and Morgan, G. (1991) Corporate Strategy, Organizations and Subjectivity: A Critique. *Organisation Studies*, **12**(2), 251–73.

Kondratiev, M. (1976) The Long Waves in Economic Life. *Lloyds Bank Review*, 41–60.

Lawrence, P. and Lorsch, J. (1967) *Organization and Environment*, Harvard Business School, Boston.

Leavy, B. and Wilson, D. (1994) *Strategy and Leadership*. Routledge, London.

Leonard-Barton, D. (1992) Core Capabilities and Core Rigidities: A Paradox in Managing New Product Development. *Strategic Management Journal*, **13**, special issue, 111–25.

Levitt, B. and March, J.G. (1988) Organizational Learning. *Annual Review of Sociology*, **14**, 319–40.

Lewin, K. (1951) *Field Theory in Social Science*, Harper and Row, New York.

Lindblom, C.E. (1959) The Science of Muddling Through. *Public Administration Review*, **19**, 79–88.

Lindblom, C.E. (1979) Still Muddling Not Yet Through. *Public Administration Review*, **39**, 517–27.

Loveridge, R. (1976) Incremental Innovation and Appropriative Learning Styles in Direct Services. In R. Loveridge and M. Pitt *The Strategic Management of Technological Innovation*, Wiley, London, 339–68.

McKiernan, P. (1995) *Strategies of Growth: Maturity, Recovery and Internationalization*, Routledge, London.

McLoughlin, I.P.M. and Harris, M. (1997) *Innovation, Organizational Change and Technology*, International Thomson Business Press, London.

Miller, D. (1992) *The Icarus Paradox*, HarperBusiness, New York.

Mintzberg, H. (1990) The Design School: Reconsidering the Basic Premises of Strategic Management. *Strategic Management Journal*, **11**(1), 171–95.

Mintzberg, H. (1994) *The Rise and Fall of Strategic Planning*, Prentice-Hall, London.

Mintzberg, H. and Quinn, J.B. (eds) (1991) *The Strategy Process, Concepts, Contexts, Cases*, Prentice-Hall, Englewood Cliffs, NJ.

Mumford, E. and Hendricks, R. (1996) Business Process Reengineering RIP. *People Management*, 2 May, 22–9.

Nelson, R.R. and Winter, S.G. (1982) *An Evolutionary Theory of Economic Change*, Harvard University Press, Cambridge, MA.

Nonaka, I. (1991) The Knowledge-Creating Company. *Harvard Business Review*, **69**(6), 96–104.

Nonaka, I. and Takeuchi, H. (1995) *The Knowledge Creating Company*. Oxford University Press, Oxford.

Oliver, N. and Wilkinson, B. (1992) *The Japanization of British Industry*, Blackwell, Oxford.

Ouchi, W.G. (1980) Markets, Bureaucracies and Clans. *Administrative Science Quarterly*, **25**, 129–41.

Peters, T. (1989) *Thriving on Chaos: Handbook for a Management Revolution*, Pan, London.

Peters, T. and Austin, N. (1985) *A Passion for Excellence*, Fontana/Collins, London.

Peters, T. and Waterman, R.H. (1982) *In Search of Excellence*, Harper and Row, London.

Pettigrew, A. (1985) *The Awakening Giant: Continuity and Change at ICI*, Blackwell, Oxford.

Pettigrew, A. and Whipp, R. (1991) *Managing Change for Competitive Success*, Blackwell, Oxford.

Pfeffer, J. (1981) *Power in Organizations*, Pitman, London.

Pfeffer, J. (1992) *Managing with Power*, Harvard Business School Press, Boston, MA.

Piore, M. and Sabel, C. (1984) *The Second Industrial Divide*, Basic Books, New York.

Polanyi, M. (1962) *Personal Knowledge: Towards a Post-Critical Philosophy*, Harper Torchbooks, New York.

Pollert, A. (ed.) (1991) *Farewell to Flexibility?* Blackwell, Oxford.

Porter, M. (1980) *Competitive Strategy*, Free Press, New York.

Porter, M. (1985) *Competitive Advantage*, Free Press, New York.

Powell, W. and DiMaggio, P.J. (1991) *The New Institutionalism in Organisational Analysis*, University of Chicago Press, Chicago.

Prahalad, C.K. and Hamel, G. (1990) The Core Competence of the Corporation. *Harvard Business Review*, **69**(3), 78–91.

Quinn, J.B. (1980) *Strategies for Change: Logical Incrementalism*, Richard D. Irwin, Chicago.

Quinn, J.B. (1982) Managing Strategies Incrementally. *Omega*, **10**(6), 613–27.

Quinn, J.B. (1991) Strategic Change: Logical Incrementalism. In H. Mintzberg and J. Quinn, *The Strategy Process: Concepts, Contexts, Cases*, Prentice-Hall, Englewood Cliffs, NJ, 96–104.

Quinn, J.B. (1992) *Intelligent Enterprise*, Free Press, New York.

Robinson, L. and Clark, P. (1997) How Do Explacite Frameworks Describe, Explain and Prescribe Hospital Infection Control? Paper prepared for Competing Through Knowledge: The Strategic and Organisational Challenge, conference at Bristol Business School, Bristol, 6–7 May.

Rumelt, R. (1994) The Evaluation of Business Strategy. In B. de Wit and R. Meyer, *Strategy: Process, Content, Context*, West, Minneapolis/St Paul, 186–92.

Rumelt, R.P., Schendel, D.E. and Teece, D.J. (1994) *Fundamental Issues in Strategy*, Harvard University Press, Cambridge, MA.

Schein, E. (1985) *Organisational Culture and Leadership*, Jossey Bass, London.

Schumpeter, J. (1939) *Business Cycles: A Theoretical, Historical and Statistical Analysis of the Capitalist Process*, McGraw-Hill, New York.

Schumpeter, J.A. (1911) *The Theory of Economic Development*, Harvard University Press, Cambridge, MA.

Scott, W.R. and Meyer, J.W. (1991) The Organization of Societal Sectors: Propositions and Early Evidence. In W. Powell and P.J. DiMaggio, *The New Institutionalism in Organisational Analysis*, University of Chicago Press, Chicago, ch. 5.

Senge, P. (1980) The Leader's New Work: Building Learning Organizations. *Sloan Management Review*, Fall, 7–23.

Sewell, G. and Wilkinson, B. (1992) Empowerment or Emasculation? Shopfloor Surveillance in a Total Quality Organisation. In P. Blyton and P. Turnbull, *Reassessing Human Resource Management*, Sage, London.

Stacey, R. (1996) *Strategic Management and Organisational Dynamics*, Pitman, London.

Stalk, G., Evans, P. and Schulman, L. (1992) Competing on Capabilities. *Harvard Business Review*, March–April, 57–69.

Starkey, K. (1996) Introduction. In K. Starkey (ed.) *How Organizations Learn*, International Thomson Business Press, London.

Starkey, K. and McKinlay, A. (1996) Product Development in Ford of Europe: Undoing the Past/Learning the Future. In K. Starkey (ed.) *How Organizations Learn*, International Thomson Business Press, London.

Starkey, K., Wright, M. and Thompson, S. (1991) Flexibility, Hierarchy, Markets. *British Journal of Management*, **2**(3), 165–76.

Storey, J. (1992) *Developments in the Management of Human Resources*, Blackwell, Oxford.

Storey, J. (ed.) (1994) *New Wave Manufacturing Strategies*, Paul Chapman, London.

Teece, D.J. (ed.) (1987) *The Competitive Challenge: Strategies for Industrial Innovation and Renewal*, Ballinger, Cambridge, MA.

Thompson, J.D. (1967) *Organizations in Action*, McGraw-Hill, New York.

Utterback, J.M. and Abernathy, W.J. (1975) A Dynamic Model Process and Product Innovation. *Omega*, **3**, 630–65.

Voss, C.A. and Robinson, S.J. (1987) Application of Just-In-Time Manufacturing Techniques in the United Kingdom. *International Journal of Operations Management*, **7**, 46–52.

Weick, K.E. (1983) Managerial Thought in the Context of Action. In S. Srivasta (ed.) *The Executive Mind*, Jossey Bass, San Francisco.

Whittington, R. (1990) The Changing Structure of R&D: From Centralisation to Fragmentation. In R. Loveridge and M. Pitt, *The Strategic Management of Technological Innovation*, Wiley, London, 183–203.

Whittington, R. (1991) The Fragmentation of Industrial R&D. In A. Pollert (ed.) *Farewell to Flexibility?* Blackwell, Oxford.

Willcocks, L. and Grint, K. (1997) Reinventing the Organization? Towards a Critique of Business Process Reengineering. In I.P.M. McLoughlin and M. Harris, *Innovation, Organizational Change and Technology*, International Thomson Business Press, London, pp. 61–86.

Williams, K., Williams, J. and Thomas, D. (1983) *Why Are the British Bad at Manufacturing*, Routledge and Kegan Paul, London.

Williamson, O. (1975) *Markets and Hierarchies: Analysis and Antitrust Implications*, Free Press, New York.

Williamson, O. (1979) Transaction-Cost Economics: The Governance of Contractual Relations. *Journal of Law and Economics*, **22**, 233–61.

Willmott, H. (1995) Will the Turkeys Vote for Christmas? The Re-engineering of Human Resources. In G. Burke and J. Peppard (eds) *Examining Business Process Re-engineering: Current Perspectives and Research Directions*, Kogan Page, London.

Wilson, D. (1992) *A Strategy of Change*, Routledge, London.

Winter, S.G. (1987) Knowledge and Competence as Strategic Assets. In D.J. Teece (ed.) *The Competitive Challenge: Strategies for Industrial Innovation and Renewal*, Ballinger, Cambridge, MA.

de Wit, B. and Meyer, R. (1994) *Strategy: Process, Content, Context*, West, Minneapolis/St Paul, 8–12.

Woodward, J. (1965) *Industrial Organization*, Oxford University Press, London.

Zuboff, S. (1988) *In the Age of the Smart Machine*, Heinemann, London.

Index